# ISTANBUL

UĞUR AYYILDIZ
Art historian and professional guide

NET
BOOKS

# CONTENTS

Published and distributed by:

**NET TURİSTİK YAYINLAR A.Ş.**

**Şifa Hamamı Sok. No. 18/2, 34400 Sultanahmet-İstanbul/Turkey**
**Tel: (90-212) 516 32 28 - 516 81 68 Fax: (90-212) 516 84 68**

**236. Sokak No.96/B Funda Apt., 35360 Hatay/İzmir/Turkey**
**Tel: (90-232) 228 78 51-250 69 22 Fax: (90-232) 250 22 73**

**Kışla Mah., 54. Sok., İlteray Apt., No.11/A-B, 07040 Antalya/Turkey**
**Tel: (90-242) 248 93 67 Fax: (90-242) 248 93 68**

**Eski Kayseri Cad., Dirikoçlar Apt. No.45, 50200 Nevşehir/Turkey**
**Tel: (90-384) 213 30 89 - 213 46 20 Fax: (90-384) 213 40 36**

Text: **Uğur Ayyıldız**
Translation: **Nüket Eraslan**
Photographs: **Şemsi Güner, Tahsin Aydoğmuş, İrfan Ertel, Erdal Yazıcı,**
**Bekir Baki Aksu, Güngör Özsoy, NET Archives**
Layout: **Not Ajans**
Typesetting: **AS&64 Ltd. Şti.**
Colour separation: **Mas Matbaacılık A.Ş.**
Printed in Turkey by: **Mas Matbaacılık A.Ş.**

**ISBN 975-479-224-0**

# WELCOME TO ISTANBUL

Located at the centre of the old world, Istanbul is an important metropolis famous for its historic monuments and magnificent scenic beauty. It is the only city in the world that expands on two continents. Situated in the region where Europe and Asia are separated by a narrow strait, the Bosphorus, it has an history of 2,500 years. Following the establishment of the city at this point of separation of the two continents where the land and sea embrace each other, the area gained strategic importance and soon became a centre for trade and commerce.

The historic city of Istanbul is located on a peninsula flanked on three sides by the Sea of Marmara, the entrance to the Bosphorus and the Golden Horn. It was the capital of three great empires: the Roman, Byzantine and Ottoman Empires. During those 1,600 years, more than 120 emperors and sultans reigned in the city. No other city in the world can claim such grandeur.

During its development, the city was enlarged four times, and each time the city walls were built more towards the west. The city of Istanbul, surrounded by the 5th century Roman city walls, spreads over seven hills, and the mosques, built by the Ottoman sultans on these hills, adorn the city as with "crowns". The skyline of the city appears serene, majestic and beautiful from every direction.

The Golden Horn, which is an unusually secure natural harbour, played a very important role in the development of the city throughout the history.

Everyday life goes on in all its vitality amid the shadows cast by the Turkish, Byzantine and Roman monuments. Istanbul is the most crowded city in Turkey. Its population is almost 8 million. It is also the most dynamic in trade, import and export, industry, entertainment, shopping and cultural activities.

The Galata district, located on the northern shore of the Golden Horn, was settled by Levantine merchants (a minority group) who controlled commerce in the city after the Byzantine era. Foreign embassies, also, used to be located in this district. Toward the end of the 19th century and the beginning of the 20th century, residential areas, European in appearance, occupied the Galata district. They still exist but the life style in these residential areas has since changed.

Commerce in the city developed over the last one hundred years along the main artery that stretches beyond Beyoğlu on the hills of Galata. New five star hotels are located on this main artery also.

Due to its location and scenic beauty, the Bos-

*Night view of Yeni Mosque.*

phorus is a wonder of nature. Typical old Turkish homes, impressive palaces, mosques, fortresses, summer residences of the foreign embassies and contemporary residences line the shores of the Bosphorus, and woods adorn the hills behind its shores. Cruises on the Bosphorus, where sail boats and row boats used tobe navigated with difficulty due to the strong currents, offer unforgettable scenery to those who take them. Because of the strong currents, experienced captains pilot the ships during their passage through the Bosphorus. The attractive Bosphorus Bridge completed in 1973, connects the two continents and blends in harmoniously with nature. The second bridge across the Bosphorus, the Fatih Bridge, was completed and opened to the traffic in 1988.

Almost one third of the population dwells in the Asian part of the city on the east shore of the Bosphorus. Hundreds of thousands of people who live on this side, use either the bridges or the ferry boats to commute to the business centre of the city.

Situated at the entrance to the Bosphorus, Üsküdar is an old residential district on the Asian side of the city. Magnificent mosques, old wooden homes and the large Selimiye Barracks, known as

*Fishermen in Eminönü.*

6

*The Ortaköy Mosque and the Bosphorus Bridge.*

the "Hospital of Florence Nightingale", are all located in this district. The area also commands the best view of the historic city. The largest cemetery in the Islamic world, the Karacaahmet Cemetery, is situated on the hills in Üsküdar.

Haydarpaşa, the railway station for the trains serving Anatolia and Asia and the main docks of the city, is situated between Üsküdar and Kadıköy.

Modern roads, beaches and yacht harbours are under construction along the shores of the Sea of Marmara.

Summer residences in well-kept gardens are found on the Princes' Islands which are only an hour away from the city by ferry. Motor vehicles are not allowed on the islands. Horse- drawn carriages are the only means of transportation. Beautiful beaches surround every island.

Known as "the smallest sea on earth", the Sea of Marmara gains access to the Aegean and the Mediterranean in the south through the Dardanelles, and to the Black Sea in the north through the Bosphorus. Many different species of fish and a rich marine flora exist in the Bosphorus.

The climate in Istanbul is ideal. Dry but not too hot summer months are followed by sunny autumn

*A Shoeshiner in front of the Yeni Mosque.*

7

*The Bosphorus Bridge.*

*The Leanders' Tower.*

*Eminönü and the Bosphorus.*

*Kumkapı: One of the locations famous for its lively night life.*

days and rainy winter months with some light snow. In the spring, especially in April and May, every shade of green and the many colours of spring flowers adorn the woods, parks and gardens in the city.

The waters of the Sea of Marmara, the Bosphorus and the Black Sea differ in salt content and temperature. It is apparent that with all these features, along with many different kinds of beaches along its shores, is Istanbul unique in the world. The Princes' Islands offer some of the best recreation spots during the summer months. In the city, there are hotels in every price range. Many five star hotels, the construction of which had been started in 1986-1987, have become operational in recent years and serve the tourists.

Restaurants serving fish, meat and other famous Turkish dishes are found everywhere in the city. The dishes prepared with fresh fish caught in the seas near the city are delectable.

Famous Turkish desserts like the baklava and other sweet pastries, particularly those produced in the small speciality shops, are prepared in the traditional way. Turkish coffee, served in demi-tasse cups, is offered on every occasion.

In spite of the population explosion in recent years and the consequent haphazard construction of new residential areas, with its historical peninsula, the Bosphorus, along the shores of which many new buildings have been built, and the Princes' Islands, which are the favorite recreation spots especially over the week-ends, Istanbul is still the most magnificent city in the world.

## TOURS OF THE CITY

The city of Istanbul, the Bosphorus, the Sea of Marmara and the Golden Horn form a unit. Nowhere else in the world such a close relationship is observed. Here reign the wonders of nature and masterpieces of human labour, and symbols of the past and the present exist together. A minimum of three to four days are required to see all these wonders. City tours leave from the ports and the hotels and last half a day. The monuments on the historic Istanbul peninsula, such as Hagia Sophia, (one of the eight wonders of the world), the Süleymaniye Mosque, the Sultanahmet Mosque, the Hippodrome and the Topkapı Palace Museum are included in the tours. Almost every tour visits the famous Covered Bazaar and its vicinity, for shopping in the spacious, modern stores.

*Hotel Merit Antique in Laleli.*

*The famous Turkish coffee.*

Limousine services are also available to visit many of the Roman, Byzantine and Turkish monuments in the city in extra comfort. To see the Roman city walls, cisterns and aqueducts, the Kariye Museum (St. Saviour in Chora), famous for its Byzantine mosaics and frescoes, the Galata Tower, the Dolmabahçe and Beylerbeyi Palaces on the Asian shore of the Bosphorus, the Archaeological Museums, the Turkish and Islamic Arts Museum (Ibrahim Paşa Palace), the Carpet Museum, the Spice Bazaar (Mısır Çarşısı), to take the cruises along the Bosphorus and to visit the Princes Islands, a long stay in Istanbul is a must. The performances by belly dancers and folk dancers add charm to evening tours. Some of the old mansions in the most crowded quarters of this historic city were restored and turned into five star hotels (like Merit Antique Hotel) in 1987.

## HISTORY OF ISTANBUL

The Aegean, the Dardanelles and the Bosphorus border the western part of Anatolia. Located near the Dardanelles, the remains of Troy is only a reminder of the past, but Istanbul, located along the shores of

11

*Aerial view of the historical peninsula and the Hagia Sophia Museum.*

the Bosphorus, is alive in all its glory and beauty, and possesses memories of the past.

There are many stories relating the foundation of the city. According to the most famous one, around 650 B.C., a tribe from the islands, under the leadership of Byzas, left their city, Megara, and began to look for a new homeland. According to the customs of the age, before any such undertaking an oracle had to be consulted. The oracle in the temple of Apollon in Delphi, the most renowned oracle of the time, advised Byzas to settle across the "land of the blind". The migrants looked for such a land for a long time. When they came to the headland of present-day Istanbul they were amazed to see such fertile lands around them, and realized the advantages offered by the Golden Horn, a natural harbour. They also noticed the people living across the stretch of water. Thinking that those people must have been blind not to see this piece of land that offered so much, Byzas and his people decided that the prophecy had come true and that they had found the land they were looking for.

However, the oldest finds discovered at the tip of the Golden Horn and in Fikirtepe on the Asiatic side, date back to 3000 B.C. It is more logical to as-

sume that the first settlement was near Kağıthane and Alibeyköy, around the tip of the Golden Horn. According to the archaeological finds and historical sources, even before the Byzas colony settled on the acropolis, a Thracian colony had lived here. Large stone blocks belonging to this colony called Lygos have been unearthed.

Since the date of its establishment, "Byzantion" existed either as an independent state or was ruled by superior powers. Where the Topkapı Palace stands today, used to be the acropolis of the city. It posssessed a well-protected harbour which is still used today. A fortified city wall, starting here, surrounded the city and reached the Sea of Marmara. In the 2nd century AD, Byzantion was a rich city located at a strategic site. Its resources included the fertile lands surrounding the city, fishery and tax collected from the ships using the Bosphorus.

During the Roman empire, Byzantion was an important sea-port and a centre for trade. It sided with the wrong party during a fight for the throne, which started in 191 A.D., and following a seige that lasted two years, it was conquered by the Roman Emperor Septimus Severus and completely destroyed. Later, the city was reconstructed and enlarged by the same

*The Pantocrator Monastery.*

emperor. New city walls were built and the city was adorned with new buildings. In the 4th century A.D. the Roman Empire expanded considerably, and Rome no longer occupied a place in the centre of the Empire. While looking for another city to move the capital to, Emperor Constantine the Great realized the strategic location, the ideal climate and the conveniences offered by the sea and land routes, and decided to move the capital here. During the next five years and more, the city was enlarged again and new city walls were constructed. Many temples, government buildings, palaces, baths and a new hippodrome were built, and in 330 A.D., the city was officially declared the capital of the Roman Empire. Many ceremonies were organized for the occasion which marked the beginning of a golden age.

Although the city was called both the Second Rome and the New Rome, these names were soon forgotten and the name Byzantion again became popular. Later, the name Constantinopolis began to be used. The name Polis was favoured by the people. Istinpolin, which means "to the city", was derived from Polis and it later became today's Istanbul.

After Constantine the Great, succeeding emperors continued to improve and embellish the city by building new avenues, business centres, aqueducts and monuments. The first churches in the city were built after Constantine.

In 395, the Roman Empire was divided into two. The Western Roman Empire collapsed in the late 5th century, but the Eastern Roman Empire, called the Byzantine Empire by modern historians, survived more than 1000 years. The Byzantine Empire, administered from Istanbul, the capital, developed under the influence of the earlier Anatolian civilizations according to the laws and regulations, and pomp and the ceremonies adopted from Rome, and most importantly by the principles and influence of Christianity. Therefore, its history is very interesting. The boundaries of the city of Istanbul were enlarged for the last time in the 5th century when the new city walls were erected. These magnificent city walls that we see today on the land side were built by Emperor Theodosius II. The reign of Emperor Justinian in the 6th century was another golden age in the history of Istanbul. The population in the city exceeded half a million, and the famous Hagia Sophia was built in this period.

The magnificent city walls, the chain that stretched across the entrance to the Golden Horn, the

Greek fire which burned even in water (only the Byzantines knew the secret), and the Byzantine diplomacy, full of intrigues, always succeeded in saving the city from attacks.

During the Iconoclastic period between 726 and 842, every kind of icon was outlawed in the city. In the 11th and 12th centuries, during the reign of the Comnenos family, Istanbul lived through another period of prosperity and progress. In 1071, the Seljouk Turks, advancing from Eastern Anatolia, succeeded in settling in Anatolia in a short time and became neighbours with the Byzantine Empire.

The Latin invasion was a dark page in the history of the city. It started with the invasion of the city by the armies of the Fourth Crusade in 1204. For many years, all the churches, monasteries and monuments in the city were robbed of their treasures. Although the Byzantines regained control of the city in 1261, Istanbul never fully recovered or regained its wealth.

The increasing threats of the expanding Ottoman Empire surrounding it finally came to an end when, following a seige of fifty-three days in 1453, the Turks entered the city. The large calibre cannons of

*Hagia Sophia Museum: the mosaic panel depicting Christ (above the entrance).*

*The Aqueduct of Valens in Saraçhane.*

14

Sultan Mehmet (the Conqueror), used for the first time in history, was one of the factors that enabled the Turks to penetrate the city walls of Istanbul. The unavoidable end of the Byzantine Empire, which was already delayed, was the other factor in the realization of the Conquest.

The Conqueror, who was only twenty-one years old then, moved the capital of the Ottoman Empire to Istanbul, increased the population in the city by bringing in immigrants from different regions in the Empire and began to reconstruct the barren city in ruins. The natives of Istanbul were granted religious and social freedom. Today, the patriarchate of the Greek Orthodox Church owes its existence to the rights granted by Sultan Mehmet then. Many of the churches in the city, starting with Hagia Sophia, were converted into mosques and saved by extensive restorations. Soon after the conquest by the Turks, the city was fully reconstructed, and one hundred years after the conquest, the unmistakable features of Turkish art became prevalent in the city, and the elegant silhouettes of minarets and domes dominated the city's skyline.

*Sultan Mehmet II, the Conqueror.*

*The repaired sections of the city walls in Topkapı.*

*Istanbul (a 19th century engraving).*

*Interior view of the Fatih Mosque.*

In the 6th century, when the Ottoman Sultans acquired the Caliphate, Istanbul became the centre of the Islamic world as well. The city was completely reconstructed by the Sultans and it acquired an eastern character. Although there are no wars recorded in the pages of Istanbul's history during this time, frequent fires devastated sections of the city.

The Imperial Palace, built where the old acropolis was, commanded an extraordinarily beautiful view of the Bosphorus and the Golden Horn. Beginning in the 19th century, mosques and palaces constructed in European style were built along the shores of the Bosphorus. Many of these palaces, built in a very short time, symbolize the decline of the Ottoman Empire. The decline of the Empire proved irreversible, and in the years following the end of World War I, the historic city, that was once Byzantium, witnessed the end of another great empire. The Ottoman Empire was split, and while the victors of the World War were engaged in a heated debate among themselves as how to divide the land, Mustafa Kemal, a noble commander in the Turkish Army, began to fight for the Turkish Nation.

Following the War of Independence, that lasted for four years, Mustafa Kemal Atatürk laid the foun-

16

dation of the Republic of Turkey in 1923 and assumed the presidency of this first republic in Asia

He led the country on the path to western civilization. The Sultan and his family were exiled, the Caliphate was abolished, the Latin alphabet was adopted, the fez, and long black garments and veil were outlawed.

By the time Atatürk died in 1938, the Turkish Republic was already recognized as a member of the western world. Although the capital of the new republic was Ankara, Istanbul was still the largest city of modern Turkey and kept its enchanting beauty and vigorous life style.

*M. Kemal Atatürk, founder of the Turkish Republic.*

*The Youth and Sports Holiday celebrations.*

# THE HIPPODROME
## (Sultanahmet Square)

The first of the seven hills on the peninsula and its extension has always been the most important and dynamic part of the city. It is known that on this acropolis, where the first settlement in the city was established, there used to be a typical Mediterranean trade centre surrounded by city walls (the boundaries of today's Topkapı Palace). Following the Roman conquest of the city, this trade centre was enlarged and reconstructed.

The most prominent monuments of the Roman era are located in the vicinity of the Hippodrome, only certain section of which are extant. The Imperial Palace known as the "Grand Palace" used to spread over the land extending from the Hippodrome down to the seashore. Only a large panel of the mosaic which used to cover the floor of one of its halls remains from this palace today. Augusteion, the most important square in the city, used to be here, and there was a victory arch between the square and the main avenue, the Milliarium. The avenue used to extend as far as Rome, and the stone marking the first kilometre was located here. Besides the palaces, baths and temples, the hippodrome, religious, cultural, social and administrative centres of the city were all located here. The area remained an important center during both the Byzantine and Turkish eras as well.

The most prominent monuments in Istanbul, such as the Hagia Sophia, the Sultanahmet Mosque, the Museum of Turkish and Islamic Arts and the Yerebatan Cistern are found in this area. The main avenues in the city (those leading down to the harbour and those extending towards the city walls in the west) started in front of the Hippodrome and followed the slopes of the hills. These were lined with business establishments and residences.

The side streets were narrow and some had steps. Side walks of some of the main avenues had two-stroyed galleries. There were wide squares along the route, and the roads leading from the squares used to fork and reach the city gates. The main avenue was called the Mese, and Via Egnetia, the road to Rome, started at the Golden Gate (Altın Kapı).

Hippodrome means "horserace track". The Roman emperor Septimius Severus built the Hippodrome towards the end of second century A.D. and Emperor Constantine the Great enlarged it to a gigantic size. According to some historians it could

seat thirty- thousand, and according to others it could seat sixty-thousand. The main attraction in the Hippodrome was two or four-horse- drawn chariot races. In the Roman era and later in the Byzantine era, the Hippodrome served as the city's main centre for meetings, entertainment and sports until the 10th century.

Like many of the other monuments in the city, the Hippodrome lost its popularity during the Latin invasion in 1204. Besides the chariot races and the gladiators, performances by musicians, acrobats and dancers used to be staged here.

For all these activities, there were many holidays in the Roman Empire.

The Hippodrome was shaped like a gigantic "U" (500 by 117 metres), and along its northern side was the Imperial Box, built like a balcony, with statues of four bronze horses on its roof. A special section with rooms and halls, separated from the public section, was connected to the Grand Palace by a passage. On the days of the performances, the emperor was in direct contact with the public.

Today, the ground level of the Hippodrome is 4-

*The Obelisque of Theodosius I.*

*The Serpent Column.*

*A view of the Hippodrome and the Sultanahmet Mosque.*

5 metres higher and three monuments stand there: the Obelisk (brought from Egypt), the Serpent Column and the Walled Obelisk. As in previous times, during the Turkish era, too, festivals and performances used to be organized in this square.

Today, the round southern section of the Hippodrome, made of a brick wall with tall arches, still exists. Most of the columns and the stone blocks of the Hippodrome were used in the construction of other structures in later periods. Today, the remains seen in the park to the right of the entrance to the Hippodrome belong to the 4th-5th century private palaces. Towards the middle of the park, the remains of a Byzantime church, Hagia Euphemia, is seen.

### The Obelisk From Egypt
### (The Obelisk of Theodosius I.)

It is one of the twin obelisks which had been erected around 1490 B.C. by Pharaoh Thutmose III in front of the temple of Karnak in Luxor to commemorate the victories of his armies in Mesopotamia. The obelisk is made of pink granite. In the 4th century, an unknown Roman emperor, wanting to accomplish something impressive to create excitement among his people, had the colossal obelisk brought to Istanbul. For years it was left lying in a corner in the Hippodrome. In 390, during the reign of Theodosius I, it was finally erected by Proclus, one of the city's administrators. This oldest monument in the city was always considered magical.

The obelisk rests on four bronze blocks on a Roman base decorated with reliefs. The emperor, his children and other important personalities watching the races from the Imperial Box, as well as musicians, dancers, certain people and races are depicted on the base. The obelisk measures 25.6 metres tall, including the base.

### The Walled Obelisk

Built of roughly cut stones, this imitation obelisk is at the southern side of the Hippodrome. The exact date of its construction is not known. It is named after Emperor Constantine Porphyrogenitus who had it repaired in the 10th century. The bronze plates, decorated with gold letters, that used to cover the obelisk were removed by the Fourth Crusaders.

### The Serpent Column

It is one of the oldest monuments in Istanbul. The heads of the three intertwined serpents formed the legs of a gold cauldron. The thirty-one Greek cities which defeated the Persians in the 5th century B.C. melted the bronze items they had captured and created this unique monument. The 8 metre high column was originally erected in the Temple of Apollon in Delphi. It was brought to Istanbul in 324 by Constantine and erected in the middle of the Hippodrome. Even by 1700, the heads of the serpents were still intact, but later they were broken off. One of them has been recovered and it is on display in the Istanbul Archaeological Museum.

### The German Fountain

The octagonal, domed fountain at the entrance to the Hippodrome was a present from the German Emperor Wilhelm II to the Sultan and the city of Istanbul. It was built in Germany in 1898, and then brought to Istanbul and installed where it stands today. Built in neo-Byzantine style, the fountain is decorated inside with gold mosaics.

# THE MUSEUM OF TURKISH AND ISLAMIC ARTS

Since 1983, the museum has occupied the 16th century building situated along the western side of Sultanahmet Square (the Hippodrome). The building used to be the palace of İbrahim Paşa. Except for the imperial palaces, it is the only extant private palace. The edifice surrounds the three sides of a terrace resting on arches, forming a courtyard in the middle. The first section of the museum is reached by a staircase from the courtyard. Rare ancient works of art created in various Islamic lands are on display in the hallways and in the rooms. Stone and baked clay objects, metal objects, ceramic and glassware, and handwritten books are some of the most valuable examples of their period. The carpets exhibited in the large halls occupying the section of the building with wide windows in the facade, are magnificent examples of the famous 13th-20th century hand-knotted Turkish carpets. This matchless collection is the richest of its kind in the world. The 13th century Seljouk carpets and rare examples from the following centuries are exhibited with much care. In the section below the carpets is the ethnographical section where everyday Turkish life and the objects used during the last few centuries are on display.

*The Museum of Turkish-Islamic Arts (below).*

*The German Fountain (above).*

22

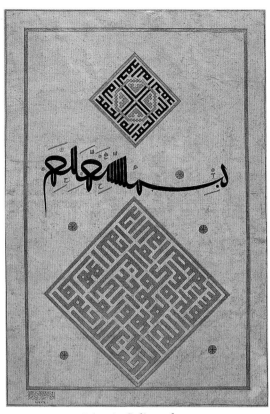

*Islamic Caligraphy..*

*A tile wall panel depicting the Kaaba.*

*A safe for the Koran.*

23

*An engraved wooden door.*

## THE SULTANAHMET MOSQUE
## (Blue Mosque)

It is the most famous monument in both the Turkish and the Islamic worlds, and it is visited by everyone who comes to Istanbul. This imperial mosque was built in the classic Turkish architectural style and it is the only mosque with six minarets. It is surrounded by other prominent edifices, built before it, in the historic city of Istanbul. Istanbul is viewed best from the sea, and Sultanahmet Mosque is part of this magnificent scenery.

Although it is popularly known as the Blue Mosque, its real name is Sultanahmet I Mosque. Befitting his real profession, its architect, Mehmet Ağa, decorated the interior fastidiously like a jeweller. Built between 1609-1616, the mosque was surrounded by a large complex of buildings for education and social activities. Some of these have collapsed in time.

There used to be a market place, Turkish baths, a public kitchen, a hospital, schools, a caravanserai and the mausoleum of Sultan Ahmet I among others. Its architect was a student of Sinan, the greatest architect of classical Turkish architecture. Here, Mehmet Ağa applied the same plan used previously by his teacher but on a larger scale.

As it is located across Hagia Sophia, the mosque was designed to be as large and as magnificent as the Byzantine structure.

The main entrance to the Sultanahmet Mosque is on the Hippodrome side. An outer courtyard surrounds the inner courtyard and the main edifice. When viewed from the inner courtyard, the domes are seen rising one above another in perfect harmony over the ablution fountain and the surrounding galleries. There are three entrances into the main chamber.

The tiles, the stained glass windows and the colourful decorations inside complement the exterior view. The interior chamber is a large unit. The central and the side domes rise above four thick columns, against which wide, pointed arches rest. Light through 260 windows illuminates the main chamber which is covered by a 43 metre-high dome. The diameter of the dome is 23 metres. The aesthetic exterior view of the domes and the facades are reflected inside.

On the walls of the balconies, surrounding the three sides of the interior, there are more than 20,000 exquisite İznik tiles. The inside of the dome and the areas above the tiles are embellished with

*Light and Sound Show in Sultanahmet Mosque.*

*An interior view of the Sultanahmet Mosque.*

paint. These painted decorations were not blue originally. The dominating blue colour, which gives its name to the mosque, was applied during later restorations.

However, during the latest restorations, completed in 1990, the interior was painted in lighter blue to attain the original colour. The floor of the mosque, as in other mosques, is covered with carpets donated.

The central chamber displays an unusually successful unity. The minber, exhibiting delicate marble work, and the chanters' balcony, supported by columns, are found in front of the mihrap. The interior offers a relaxing and ethereal atmosphere where crowds of believers worship in pious reverence.

The exterior view of the edifice has a pyramidal appearance due to a series of domes arranged from higher to lower. Six minarets, four at the corners and two outside the inner courtyard, complement the beautiful appeearence.

The Imperial Pew is connected to the two- storeyed pavilion, outside, by a ramp. The pavilion, where the Sultan used to rest, today houses the rich Carpet Museum of the Administration of Pious Foundation.

*An interior view of the Sultanahmet Mosque.*

The market place, which has been restored in recent years, is on the east side of the edifice. The single domed, large mausoleum of Sultan Ahmet and the school buildings are located on the side facing Hagia Sophia.

Light and Sound Shows are put on in the park here during the summer.

The Sultanahmet Mosque, with the monumental edifices and the museums in its vicinity, is the focal point of city tours.

*The Mausoleum of Ahmet II.*

# THE MUSEUM OF CARPETS AND KILIMS

The Administration of Pious Foundations of the Turkish Republic owns an extensive collection of old carpets and kilims, but only a part of this collection is displayed.

The carpets are exhibited in the Sultan's Pavilion in the Sultanahmet Mosque, and the kilims in the vaulted lower galleries entered through the rear gardens of the mosque. Best examples of 14th-20th century Turkish carpets are exhibited along the ramp, which is the entrance to the pavilion, and in the rooms where the Sultan used to rest. The carpets and kilims on display have been repaired and are displayed in a contemporary fashion.

# THE MOSAIC MUSEUM

The marketplace behind the Sultanahmet Mosque is situated on the remains of an old palace dated between the 4th and 6th centuries. The mosaics of the palace were discovered at the lower end of the mar-

*The Carpet and Kilim Museum and two old carpets exhibited in the museum.*

ket, in their original places. It is known that these mosaics, unearthed in the 1930s, used to decorate the floor of a large hall in the palace. These mosaic panels, which depict hunting scenes, scenes from everyday life, and impressive decorative designs exhibit high quality workmanship.

Buds encircled by bent acanthus leaves, a Medusa head and scenes from a lion hunt are some of the most attractive examples. Scenes depicted in these mosaic panels, created in the style of Antakya Mosaic School (Roman Age), are extremely realistic.

Due to the discovery of the mosaic panels of an old palace here other mosaics unearthed in the other sections of the city were framed by concrete panels and brought here to be displayed. Restoration of the market place has been completed and the Mosaic Museum has been reopened to the public.

*Two mosaic panels exhibited in the Mosaic Museum.*

*The Hagia Sophia Museum.*

# THE HAGIA SOPHIA MUSEUM

Hagia Sophia, which is considered one of the eight wonders of the world, is the most prominent building in History of Art and world architecture. It is one of those rare structures, that, in spite of its age and large size, is still in very good condition. Turks call it Aya Sofya. It is erroneously known as Saint Sophia. The basilica was dedicated to Divine Wisdom and not to a saint named Sophia. Its name means Holy Wisdom. Two other basilicas had been built here, the site of an old pagan temple, and they were all known by the same name. Although no churches were built during the reign of Constantine the Great, certain sources indicate that the first basilica at the site had been built by him.

The first basilica of Hagia Sophia was small in size and had a wooden roof. It was built in the second half of the 4th century by Constantinius, son of Constantine the Great. When it was burned during the riots in 404, a larger basilica was built to replace it, and this second church was opened for services in 415 by a ceremony. In 532, during the riots that started following a chariot race in the Hippodrome, tens of thousands of people lost their lives and many buildings were burned and destroyed; among these was the second Hagia Sophia. This rebellion, known as the Nika Revolt, was directed against Emperor Justinian. When he finally suppressed the riots, he decided to build a monument that would surpass all the existing monuments. Construction started in 532 over the remains of the previous basilica and was completed in five years. Elaborate ceremonies were organized for the dedication of this, the largest church in the Christian world, in 537. The emperor spared no expense and placed the state treasury at the disposal of architect Anthemius of Tralles and the famous mathematician, Isidorus of Miletus who were in charge of the construction of the edifice.

The plan of the basilica was not original, and the dome was constructed according to a style developed previously by the Romans.

Large round buildings had been successfully covered by domes before, but Hagia Sophia had a rectangular floor plan, and covering a large rectangular structure by a huge central dome was being tried for the first time in history. While the priests prayed, the construction progressed. Many different kinds of marble, and columns from the remains of ancient structures in every corner of the empire were

brought and used in the construction. Later, many stories were made up to describe the origin of the materials, especially the columns. Justinian had built Hagia Sophia to please himself and for prestige, but in the following centuries it became a legend and a religious symbol.

Despite its magnificence, Hagia Sophia had many structural problems. The enormous size of the dome and the stress it exerted on the side walls were the most important factors to consider. Architectural elements necessary to transmit the weight of such a large dome to the foundation had not yet been fully developed. The side walls that kept leaning outwards finally caused the collapse of the original dome in 558. The second dome was taller but smaller in diameter, yet almost half of this dome, too, collapsed in the 10th century and then again in the 14th century. Hagia Sophia was kept standing by spending vast sums of money in every age, and due to lack of money in the treasury of the Byzantine Empire towards the end, the church was left to ruins. It was the conquest of Istanbul by Turks under Sultan Mehmet the Conqueror, and the subsequent conversion of Hagia Sophia into a mosque, that saved this beautiful monument. The Turkish master architect, Sinan the Great (Koca Sinan), built the buttresses outside, in the 16th century.

Hagia Sophia, which had served for 916 years as a church and 477 years as a mosque, was turned into a museum on Atatürk's orders. Between 1930 and 1935, some of the mosaics in the edifice were cleaned of the whitewash covering them. They are among the most important works of art that have survived to this day of the Byzantine era.

The original atrium of the edifice is not extant. The columns and other relics seen at the entrance are placed here for exhibit.

The entrance is from the courtyard and it entered faces west. This is the original entrance which had not been used for centuries. Next to the entrance are the remains of the earlier (the second) basilica. The people who were not baptized could enter the outer hallway (exonarthex) from where five doors lead into the inner narthex, and from here, nine doors lead into the nave. The tall door in the middle was the Imperial Entrance. The mosaic panel seen above it is dated to the end of the 9th century. In the centre of the panel is Christ the Pantocrator, sitting on a throne, and next to him is an emperor pleading for divine mercy. On both sides of the throne there are roundels. One of them has the figure of the Virgin Mary and the other the Archangel Gabriels. The nonfigurative mosaic on the ceiling of the inner nar-

*Virgin Mary and the Christ-Child: on the left, Emperor Commenos II and on the right, Empess Irene.*

thex dates back to the reign of Justinian.

The magnificent nave is overwhelming. The dome's presence is felt as soon as one enters the nave. It appears as though suspended in the air and covers the whole building. The walls and the ceilings which are covered with marble and mosaics create a colourful appearance. The three different tones of colour observed in the mosaic decorations of the dome indicate the three different restorations. With its height and the size of its diameter it is one of the largest domes in the world. The dome is not perfectly round any more due to various restorations. Its diameter measures 31.87 metres from north to south and 30.87 metres from east to west. Four-winged angels, with their faces covered, are depicted on the four pendentives which support the dome. Mosaics depicting some of the church leaders are seen on the northern wall above the galleries. These were made at a later date.

Columns separate the rectangular middle nave from the side naves. The central nave measures 74.67 metres by 69.80 metres and there are altogether 107 columns, including those on the ground floor and in the galleries.

The marble column capitals were carved deep to bring out better the effects of light and shadow, and the elegant acanthus leaves blend with the volutes. These were some of the features of contemporary Byzantine art. The imperial monograms are seen on the capitals.

A mosaic panel depicting the Virgin and the Christ - Child is seen on the semi- dome of the apse. On each side wall there was a figure of an angel. One of them is completely missing and the other is partially extant. Huge leather medallions, 7.5 metres in diameter and with inscriptions on them, are seen on the walls at the gallery level. These and the inscriptions on the dome remind the visitors of its days as a mosque. On the medallions are the names of Prophet Mohammed, the first four caliphs, the two grandchildren of the prophet, Hasan and Hüseyin, and the word "God". These are the works of master calligraphers of the mid-19th century.

The "mihrab" (niche indicating the direction of Mecca) in the apse, the "minber" (pulpit to the right of the mihrab used during the Friday prayer), and the raised platform for the chanters (mevlithanlar balkonu) were placed in the nave in the Turkish era.

The stained glass windows of the apse have inscriptions, and they are outstanding examples of their kind. A ramp inside the first northern buttress gives access to the upper galleries. The magnificent central nave appears completely different when seen from the galleries on its three sides. In the galleries, there were sections reserved for the ladies of the imperial family and the meetings of the church council. In the northern gallery there is only one mosaic panel, but in the southern gallery there are three panels each depicting a different figure: the Virgin, Christ, members of the imperial family. The floor of the galleries is uneven due to damage caused by earthquakes and regular use. The southern gallery was divided into two by a door-like ornate marble divider at a later date. The inner section was used during the meetings of the church council.

The first mosaic panel seen here is considered the most beautiful mosaic not only in Hagia Sophia but also in the art of mosaic (late 13th century). In the Christian world, the Last Judgement was the most crowded scene painted. It was always depicted with many figures, and with Jesus Christ in the centre. In this panel, He is seen in the centre with the Virgin on His right and St. John the Baptist on His left,

*Interior view of the Hagia Sophia Museum.*

*An interior view of the Hagia Sophia Museum.*

forming a group of three. The scene is called the "Deesis" and depicts the pleading for the salvation of mankind. Although the mosaic pieces of the lower section of the panel have fallen off, the upper sections of the figures are in good shape.

At the far end of the southern gallery there are two panels. Five figures are depicted in the first one. The Virgin, with the Christ-Child in her lap, is seen in the centre of the panel. Emperor Comnenus is on the left and Empress Eirene is on the right. On the side wall next to the panel, the ailing Prince Alexius is depicted. The offerings of the members of the palace are depicted in this 12th century mosaic.

In the second panel, Christ, sitting on a throne and holding the holy book in one hand, is depicted in a gesture of benediction. Empress Zoe and her husband Emperor Constantine Monomachus are also depicted in the panel. Emperor Constantine was Empress Zoe's third husband. This is why the inscriptions above of the mosaic panel and the head of the figure depicting her husband were redone.

The scroll and the bag presented to Jesus symbolize independence and the offerings. On the pillar at

*Virgin Mary and the Christ-Child.*

*Virgin Mary, Christ and St. John the Baptist.*

*An interior view of the Basilica Cistern.*

the end of the northern gallery, there is a mosaic panel depicting Prince Alexander (10th century). The large panel seen while leaving the inner narthex belongs to the 10th century. The figures with distorted perpectives represent the Virgin and the Christ-Child in the centre, Constantine the Great, (presenting the model of Istanbul walls), and Justinian, presenting the model of Hagia Sophia), on each side.

## THE YEREBATAN CISTERN
## (The Basilica Cistern)

The largest and the most magnificent covered cistern in Istanbul is entered through a small building to the west of Hagia Sophia Square. The ceiling of this forest of columns is made of brick and is cross-vaulted. A street runs above a section of the cistern. Due to a basilica once situated on the cistern, it is known as the Basilica Cistern. It was built in the reign of Constantine I and repaired and enlarged in the reign of Justinien I (527-565). It supplied water to the palace complex nearby.

There are twenty-eight columns in each of the twelve rows of columns (a total of 336), and the cistern measures 140 metres by 70 metres. Some of the

*The Medusa head in the Basilica Cistern.*

*A view of the Archeological Museum.*

*The Lician Sarcophagus.*

columns have plain but most of them have Corinthian capitals. The water level in the cistern changed from season to season. There are pipes at different levels in the eastern wall and water used to be distributed through these pipes. The traces left by different levels of water can be seen on the columns.

During the restoration project initiated in 1984, the bottom of the cistern was scraped, and when the two-metre deep mud was removed, the original brick pavement was brought to light. Also, two Medusa heads which serve as column base have been discovered.

## ISTANBUL ARCHAEOLOGICAL MUSEUMS

In the first courtyard of TopkapıPalace, are the Museum of Oriental Antiquities, the Archaeological Museum and the Tiled Pavilion (Çinili Köşk). These are collectively called Istanbul Archaeological Museums. In these museums 60.000 archaeological finds, 760.000 coins and 75.000 clay tablets are displayed. With such rich collections, collectively they are the richest in Turkey and among the few in the world.

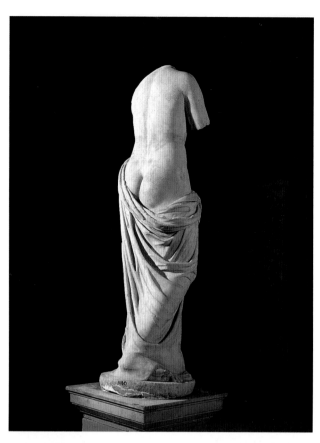

*Statue of a Nymph (above). Bust of Emperor M. Aurelius.*

# THE ARCHAEOLOGICAL MUSEUM

It was founded by the famous painter, archaeologist Osman Hamdi Bey and opened to the public on June 13, 1891 under the name of Müze-i Hümayun (the Imperial Museum). In 1902 and 1908, new wings were added on to the building and on June 13, 1991, on the centennial of the founding of the museum, it was reopened to the public after being rearranged. The monumental gate of this building was designed by architect Valaury.

At the entrance is the huge and scary statue of God Bess. In the halls to the right of the entrance, examples of "Antique Age Sculpture" are exhibited. Unique examples of sculpture from the Archaic age until the end of Roman era are exhibited in separate halls called "Antique Grave Stones and Reliefs", "Treasures from Persian Reign in Anatolia", Kenan Erim Hall (Aphrodisias Finds), "Three Marble Cities in Anatolia" (Ephesus, Miletus, Aphrodisias), "Hellenistic Sculpture", "Magnesia AD Meandrum and Tralles (Aydın) Statue Group", "Hellenistic and Hellenistic Influenced Roman Sculpture", "Roman Sculpture".

Following the counters, where souvenirs and books are sold, on the left of the entrance, is the hall dedicated to Osman Hamdi, founder of the museum. Right after this hall, treasures unearthed during the excavation of the Royal Cemetery in Sidon are exhibited. Excavation of the cemetery was carried on by Osman Hamdi, himself.

The first of the three sarcophagi standing side by side belongs to Tabnit, the king of Sidon. A unique Lician sarcophagus and a Satrap sarcophagus are also found in this hall. Then come the world famous Sarcophagus of Alexander the Great and the Sarcophagus of the Mourning Women. Both of these were discovered during the excavation of the Royal Cemetery in Sidon, and they date back to the 4th century B.C..

On the sides of the Sarcophagus of Alexander the Great are reliefs depicting hunting scenes and scenes from the war between the Hellens and the Persians.

Various architectural fragments are displayed in the annex building. In the ground floor is the hall of "Antique Age Anatolian Architecture" and in the first storey is the hall of "Istanbul Through the Centuries". On the second storey, small archaeological finds belonging to the Paleolithic age, Early, Middle and Late Bronze Ages and the Phyrigian State Age in Anatolia are displayed under the heading "Anatolia Through the Centuries and Troy". A section of this hall is reserved for the artifacts found in Troy,

*Sarcophagus of Mourning Women (Above).*

*Sarcophagus of Alexander the Great (Detail).*

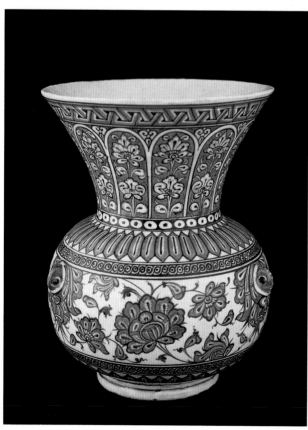

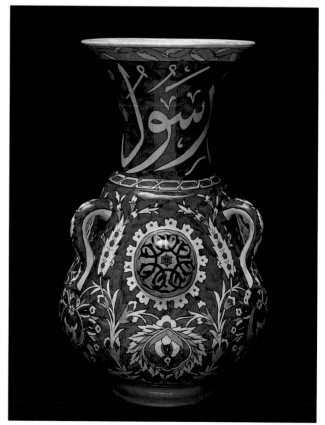

*Hall of the Roman Sculpture (above).*

*İznik Oil lamps (in the shape of a vase), (below).*

and the treasures discovered in the settlements I-IX are displayed in separate showcases.

Various objects found in the graves belonging to the Phyrigian State civilization are also displayed on this storey. On the third storey, under the heading of "Civilizations in Anatolia and the Neighbouring Lands", treasures discovered in Cyprus, Palestine and Syria are displayed in chronological order

## The Museum of Oriental Antiquities

The building located to the left of the entrance of the Archaeological Museum first housed the Academy of Fine Arts which was founded by Osman Hamdi Bey in 1883. In 1917, the Academy was relocated to another building in the Cağaloğlu district and the original building was given to the Archaeological Museum. To exhibit the relics from the Near and Middle Eastern cultures, a separate section was established by the Archaeological Museum and this exhibition was moved to the building of the Academy. The two large basalt lions seen at the entrance to the museum are Neo-Hittite.

The exhibition halls in the upper storey are arranged in a contemporary fashion. Treasures gathered from the lands under the Ottoman rule before World War I are displayed here. This is a unique museum where invaluable relics belonging to ancient Anatolian Civilizations are exhibited together.

Besides the relics that belong to the Old and New Sumerians, graves of the pharoahs, relics from pre-Islamic Arabian cultures, and Assyrian and Babylonian civilizations are on display. There are also impressive collections of relics belonging to the Hittite-Hatti and Urartian civilizations in Anatolia.

## The Tiled Pavilion (Çinili Köşk)

It is the first pavilion built by Mehmet the Conqueror in 1472 to be used in the summers. With its facades decorated with columns, arches and a balcony, its antechamber and tile wall decorations, it exhibits the characteristics of early Ottoman architecture, which was under the influence of Seljouk architecture. The antechamber at the entrance is decorated with a multi-coloured, long inscription created with cut tiles. The central chamber has a dome and it is surrounded by vaulted rooms. The 12th-20th century Seljouk and Ottoman ceramics and tiles are exhibited in chronological order. Beautiful tiles from the famous 16th century İznik workshops constitute one of the most important collections in the museum.

*The Museum of Ancient Orient and the Tiled Pavilion.*

A procession in the Sultanahmet Square (above).

44

Two Ottoman miniatures (below).

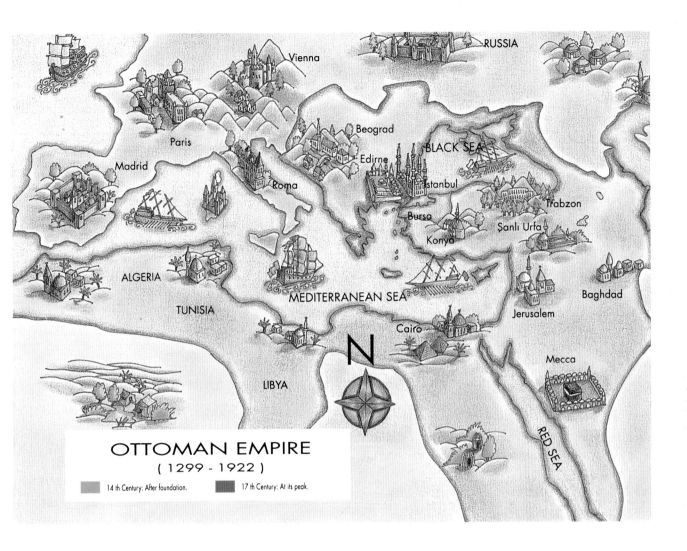

OTTOMAN EMPIRE
( 1299 - 1922 )

14 th Century: After foundation.    17 th Century: At its peak.

# THE OTTOMAN EMPIRE

Central Asia was the homeland of Turks. Over the centuries, they either migrated in large groups or organized military expeditions to various regions in Asia and even to Central Europe. Early in the 7th century, these nomadic Turkish tribes began to settle and establish states.

The most important one was the small Seljouk tribe in Asia Minor which grew into the powerful Ottoman Empire that lasted for six hundred years. Although the Ottomans constituted the minority in the lands they conquered, due to their superior ability to organize and administer efficiently, they governed these lands successfully. They provided a secure and peaceful life for their subjects (Jews, Christians and Moslems) regardless of race, religion, culture or nationality.

The reign of Süleyman the Magificent was the golden age of the empire. For almost four hundred years, the Ottoman Empire ruled lands in Europe, Africa and Asia Minor extending from Russia, and Persia to the Balkans, Greece and as far as Vienna.

Towards the end of the 19th century, different nations under the Ottoman rule, agitated by foreign powers, began to revolt, thereby weakening the internal structure of the empire.

World War I was the final blow that brought on the collapse of the Ottoman Empire along with its allies.

The lands of the empire were divided among the victors, but Kemal Atatürk led the Turkish nation to victory after a war for independence, and founded the Republic of Turkey in 1923.

*A Sultan scattering gold coins in front of the Baghdat Pavilion (above). Ceremony in front of the Gate of Akağalar.*

# THE TOPKAPI PALACE MUSEUM

The Topkapı Palace where the Ottoman Sultans lived for many years, in 1924, was turned into a museum upon the orders of Atatürk. Situated on the Acropolis hill, which was the site of the first settlement in Istanbul, the palace commands an impressive view of the Golden Horn, the Bosphorus and the Sea of Marmara. It is located at the tip of the peninsula of old Istanbul, and is a complex surrounded by five kilometer long walls and occupies an area of 700,000 m². Following the conquest of the city in 1453, the young conqueror, Sultan Mehmet, declared Istanbul the capital of the Ottoman Empire.

The first palace he built in the city was located in the middle of the town. The second palace he built in 1470s was originally called the New Palace but later it came to be known as the Topkapı Palace. Just like the other historic Turkish palaces, Topkapı Palace is a classic Turkish palace complex which consists of courtyards, shaded with trees and serving different purposes, and are separated from each other by monumental gates. Pavilions, each used for a different purpose, surround these courtyards. Since its first construction, the palace has been altered and enlarged by new additions in the reign of each succeeding sultan. In 1853, when the sultans moved into the Dolmabahçe Palace, the Topkapı Palace was abandoned. As a palace it was quite different from other palaces since it was used for multiple purposes. Besides being the official residence of the Sultan, the sole ruler of the Empire, the Topkapı Palace served as the headquarters of the government where the ministers met. It also housed the state treasury and the archives. The mint, as well as the highest educalional institution, the University of the Sultan and the State were located the palace grounds. Therefore, the Palace was the heart, the brain, i.e. the very centre of the Ottoman Empire. Later, the private harem of the Sultan was moved here, too.

Thirty-six sultans reigned during the Ottoman Empire, and in the 16th century, when the sultans acquired the Caliphate, they became the religious leaders of the Islamic world.

Capable civil servants, after completing their education in the school in the private courtyard of the sultan, served faithfully and successfully in the administration and organization of the vast empire. Many of the viziers and grand viziers were gradu-

*An aerial view of the Topkapı Palace.*

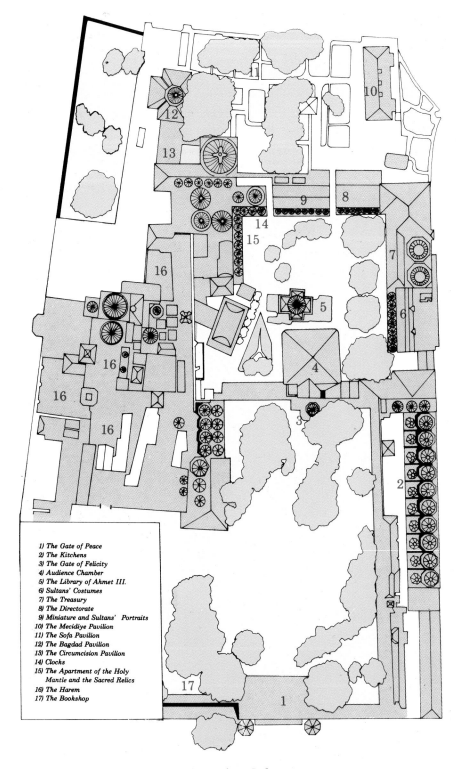

1) The Gate of Peace
2) The Kitchens
3) The Gate of Felicity
4) Audience Chamber
5) The Library of Ahmet III.
6) Sultans' Costumes
7) The Treasury
8) The Directorate
9) Miniature and Sultans' Portraits
10) The Mecidiye Pavilion
11) The Sofa Pavilion
12) The Bagdad Pavilion
13) The Circumcision Pavilion
14) Clocks
15) The Apartment of the Holy
    Mantle and the Sacred Relics
16) The Harem
17) The Bookshop

Plan of the Topkapı Palace.

The Gate of Felicity, the second gate of the Topkapı Palace.

Soğukçeşme Street and the Fountain of Ahmet III.

*The Church of Hagia Eirene.*

*The Tower of Justice and Kubbealtı.*

ates of this school. Life in the palace was very strict and started at dawn. It was ceremonious and was dictated by the strict rules of protocol. Everybody was required to abide by the centuries-old customs and traditions, even during the decline of the empire. The protocol applied here influenced the rules of protocol in the Western world.

The seaside mansions and the pavilions of the Topkapı Palace complex were in ruins towards the of the last century. The different kinds of tiles and woodwork, and architectural styles displayed in the Topkapı Palace complex demonstrate the different stages of the development of Turkish art, and the harmonious existence of different styles.

## THE FIRST COURTYARD

The Imperial Gate (Bab-ı Hümayun) leads into the First Courtyard. The monumental fountain seen outside the gate is a beautiful example of 18th century Turkish art. The palace bakery, the mint, the quarters of the palace guards and the firewood depots surrounded this courtyard. Private vegetable gardens used to be on the terraces below. The first pavilion built on the grounds of Topkapı Palace was

the Tiled Pavilion (Çinili Köşk) and it was built in this courtyard. Hagia Eirene Museum (Aya Irini) is a 6th century Byzantine church, and it is seen on the left upon entering the courtyard.

## THE SECOND COURTYARD

The main entrance to Topkapı Palace Museum is through the second gate known as the Gate of Salutation which opens onto the second courtyard. This courtyard was the administration center of the state, and here, only the sultan was allowed to ride on horseback. Only citizens with official business, and representatives of the Janissary Corps on paydays were admitted into this coutyard.

Foreign representatives were received, and state ceremonies were organized here. Even during ceremonies attended by five or ten thousand people absolute silence prevailed. When the sultan himself attended the ceremonies, the imperial throne was placed in front of the gate seen at the other end of the courtyard and as a demonsration of respect, those present used to stand with hands clasped in front.

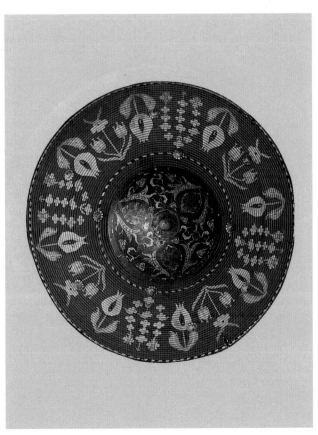

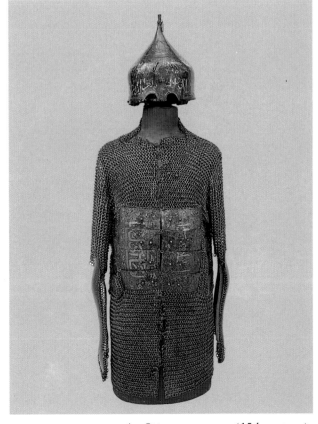

*The Gate of Akağalar (above). A decorated shield.*

51

*An Ottoman armour (15th century).*

## THE WEAPONS COLLECTION

The section next to the "Divan Room" with wide eaves used to house the state treasury. The building which resembles a large hall has eight domes and today it houses the weapons collection. The collections have been rearranged in a contemporay fashion and the building reopened to the public. Besides the armours and weapons used by the sultans, those used by the members of the palace are also on exhibit along with the weapons used by the Turkish army in different periods. In this very rich collection, weapons of other nations, acquired as booty, are also exhibited. The section where the governing officials met is on the left side of the courtyard. The only tower in the palace is located here, too. Since this was the state court of justice, the tower is known as the Tower of Justice.

## THE KITCHENS AND PORCELAIN SECTION

The palace kitchens are on the right side of the second courtyard. The building housing the kitchens has twenty chimneys. From the second courtyard,

*A section of the showcase of the Japanese porcelains.*

*A blue-white plate, the Ming Dynasty.*

52

*A blue-white plate, the Ming Dynasty.*

three gates open onto the Kitchens Section. The buildings housing the kitchens are located along both sides of a long street paved with stone. In the Helvahane (Sweet Paistry) section of the Kitchens, objects such as pots, pans, trays, bowls, pitchers and coffee grinders, which were used in every day life by the members of the palace, are displayed. More than one -thousand master chefs and their assistants used to prepare meals for the occupants of the different sections of the palace. Of the 12,000 pieces of Chinese and Japanese porcelain, about 2,500 are exhibited. The porcelain collection which is exhibited in chronological order, is one of the richest in the world. The unique Chinese celadons are exhibited to the right of the entrance, in the first hall. Blue and white, and mono - and polychrome porcelains are followed by the Japanese porcelains in the last section of the exhibition. Certain sections of the kitchens have been kept in their original condition. The porcelain and glassware produced in Istanbul are exhibited in another section. Opposite the kitchens are the Silverware and European Porcelains, and Crystal Section which was opened in 1985. At the end of the

*A hall with a fireplace, the Harem.*

*The Imperial Hall.*

*The Fruit Room, the Harem.*

*Abdülhamit I Pavilion and the quarters of the Concubines.*

alley that leads to the kitchens, there is a colossal Early Byzantine column in the Corinthian order

## THE HAREM

Until the 16th century, the Harem was housed in the Old Palace in the middle of the city. The Harem of Topkapı Palace consists of long and narrow hallways surrounded by high walls, and approximately four hundred rooms scattered around small courtyards. It was altered and enlarged by additions built in different periods. The Sultan's mother, his brothers and sisters and the other members of the Imperial family had private quarters in the Harem. Many concubines and eunuchs served this big family The Harem, which was like the private section of a home, could rarely be entered by an outsider. Many stories have been told over the centuries about this very private section of the palace. The concubines serving the Sultan and his family were chosen among the most beautiful and healthy girls of different races and presented as gifts to the palace. These young girls, barely out of childhood, were educated according to the strict rules of the Harem. After they became thoroughly acquainted with the customs and traditions in the palace, they were separated into groups. Those who could attract the attention of the Sultan had the chance of becoming even his wife. The title "Empress" was not used in the empire. The Sultan's mother (Valide Sultan) ruled the Harem. Amid all the splendour and wealth, rivalry, intrigues and struggles to get closer to the Sultan were part of daily life. When a new sultan ascended the throne, the harem of the former sultan used to be moved to the Old Palace. The ladies of the Harem and the chief eunuchs would emerge as a political power influencing the state's administration if the reigning sultan had a weak character or could not exert authority. Life in the Harem, with all its pomp, ugliness and intrigues, was still superior to the life style of contemporary ladies.

Today, only a certain section of the Harem is open to the public. In contrast to the lively old days, the dim hallways and empty rooms today leave a lot to the visitor's imagination. The rooms, ceilings and the hallways in the Harem are lavishly decorated. Tiles of different periods are seen side by side here. A visit to the Harem starts at the quarters of the Sultan's Mother, and the section with forty rooms. A large Turkish bath and the spacious, domed private

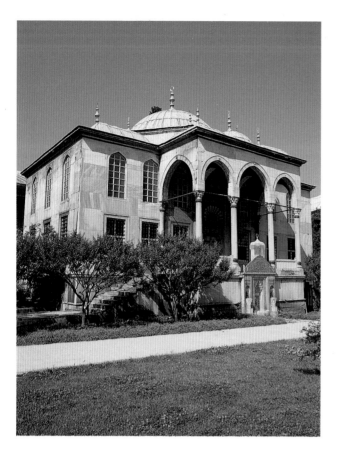

hall of the sultans are found here. There are fireplaces and fountains in every room of importance.

The room of Murat III in the Harem is a large room famous for its 16th century tiles and recessed fountains with a pool. The small library entered through here, the Fruit Room (Yemiş Odası), has very interesting wall paintings depicting fruit and flowers. The two consecutive 16th century rooms seen towards the end of the tour of the Harem have beautiful stained glass windows complementing the rich wall decorations. These rooms were reserved for the Crown Princes and they are called "Double Pavilions".

## THE THIRD COURTYARD

The Gate of Felicity (Babussaade) leads into the third courtyard. Only those with a special permission could enter through this gate guarded by the White Eunuchs. The third courtyard was reserved for the sultan. The Imperial University, the Throne Room, the private treasury of the sultan, and the quarters housing the sacred relics were located in this section of the palace. The sultans used to re-

*The Library of Ahmet III.*

*The Throne Room.*

56

ceive the foreign ambassadors and meet with the government officials in the Throne Room. Those serving in the Throne Room, were deaf and mute for security reasons. Officers of the Ottoman army, who were also prominent members of the imperial school, used to serve the sultans.

The Library of Sultan Ahmet III is in the centre of the courtyard. This 18th century building displays a style which is a blend of baroque and Turkish architectural styles.

## THE SULTANS' COSTUMES SECTION

A collection of the sultans' costumes are exhibited in the section on the right side of the third courtyard. It is unique in the world. Since the 15th century, these handmade costumes, made of fabric woven on the palace looms, have been preserved with great care in accordance with the old tradition of saving the costumes of the sultans and other pominent state officials in special wraps and placing them in their mausoleums.

Besides the costumes embroidered with silk, gold and silver threads, silk prayer rugs are also on display. These prayer rugs, each one a masterpiece of

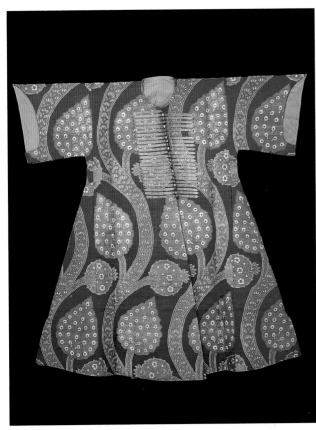
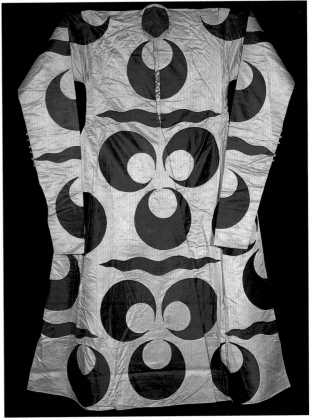

*Three different sultan caftans.*

the Turkish art of weaving, were the private rugs of the sultans.

## THE TREASURY SECTION

The Treasury section of Topkapı Palace Museum is the richest of its kind. All the pieces exhibited in the four halls are authentic. Masterpieces of the Turkish art of jewellery of different centuries, and exquisite creations from the Far East, India and Europe are fascinating. In each exhibition hall there is an imperial throne used during a different period of the empire. Ceremonial attire and accessories, weaponry, water pipes, Turkish coffee cups and other containers decorated with gold and precious stones are the most significant items in the first hall. The gold plated silver model of a Chinese palace displays delicate craftsmanship. The figurine depicting a man enjoying a water pipe under a canopy is another well known piece in the first hall. This unique piece, embellished with jewels, exhibits superior gold and enamel workmanship. A baroque pearl forms the body of the figure. It was sent as a present to Sultan Abdülaziz from India in the 19th century.

The second hall is known as the Emerald Room.

*The Topkapı dagger.*

*Quiver embroidered with gold medalion designs.*

*A ceremonial helmet.*

Very attractive aigrettes and pendants, decorated with emeralds and other precious stones, are displayed here. Uncut emeralds weighing a few kilograms each, and the Topkapı Dagger (symbol of the museum), embellished with four large emeralds, are also on display. The dagger is an excellent example of 18th century Turkish jewellery. It is plated with enamel and embellished with rosecut diamonds. There is a big emerald on the lid of the watch found at the tip of the hilt.

In the third hall, enamelled objects, medals and decorations presented to the sultans by foreign nations, the twin solid gold candelabras, each weighing 49 kilograms, and the most famous throne in the palace, the golden throne used during coronations and on religious holidays, are on display. One of the largest diamonds in the world, the Spoonseller Diamond (Kaşıkçı Elması), also known as the Pigot Diamond, is displayed in a special showcase in the hall. The origin of this dazzling diamond is not known. According to a rumour, it got its name from a spoonseller who traded it for a few wooden spoons. Sources indicate that in 1774, in India, an officer in

*The Spoonseller's Diamond.*

*A crystal canteen (16th century)*

59

*A ceremonial canteen (16th century).*

*The entrance to the Sacred Relics Section.*

the French army whose name was Pigot, purchased a diamond matching the size and shape of this diamond. After changing hands a few times, it was sold to a governor in Turkey by the mother of Napoleon Boneparte. Fortynine smaller diamonds surround this special, 86 carat rose-cut diamond.

A balcony, which commands a magnificent view of the Bosphorus and the Asiatic coast, connects the third and the fourth halls. The impressive throne of Turko-Indian origin is displayed in the fourth hall.

Relics said to have belonged to St. John the Baptist are seen in the first showcase in the hall. Chess sets, pill boxes, chests of drawers and weapons, decorated with jewels, are some of the most beautiful objects on display.

### THE SACRED RELICS

Following the conquest of Egypt in early 16th century, the sacred relics of Islam were brought to the Palace, they have been kept at this section since then. It is assumed that this hall, at the corner of the third courtyard, used to be the Throne Room before the relics were stored here. The walls of the hall with domes are covered with tiles. The swords of

*Privy chamber (above). The sword of Caliph Osman.*

*Portrait of Sultan Beyazıd II.*

Mohammed, his bow and his mantle (stored in a large gold box) are in the inner room. The huge canopy in this room, viewed only through a single window, is made of silver. In the other room, belongings of the Prophet (his seal, a few hairs from his beard, a letter and his footprint) are exhibited in showcases. One of the first handwritten copies of the Koran, the keys to the Kaaba in Mecca, and the swords of prominent people are some of the sacred objects on exhibit.

### THE SULTANS' PORTRAITS AND GALLERY

Between the Sacred Relics Section and the Treasury Section, there is a colonnade. The Portraits Section is located in the section next to the offices of the museum along this colonnade. In the large hall here, different exhibitions are organized from time to time. In the Topkapı Palace Museum there are many rich collections of manuscripts, books, miniatures, writing tools and many other priceless objects in storage. From time to time these rare

*Portrait of Sultan Selim III.*

*Portrait of Yavuz Sultan Selim. (Above)*

items are shown to the public through displays arranged in this exhibition hall. There is a balcony-like gallery in the hall and portraits of the Sultans are seen hanging on the walls in this gallery.

## THE CLOCKS SECTION

The richest collection of clocks in the world is on display in this section next to the Sacred Relics Section in the third courtyard. On the right side of the entrance, the works of Turkish master watchmakers are displayed. Priceless wall and table clocks, and watches produced between the 16th and late 19th centuries make up the rest of the exhibition. All of these are foreign made and they were presentend to the palace as gifts. The biggest clock in the hall is British made and has an organ. It is 3.5 metre tall and 1 metre wide. Among the pocket watches, the ones with the portrait of Sultan Abdülmecit and Abdülaziz are quite interesting.

## THE FOURTH COURTYARD

Passageways lead from the third courtyard into

*An Ottoman wall clock.*

*A pocket watch with a portrait of Sultan Abdülaziz.*

*The interior of Baghdad Pavilion.*

*Baghdad Pavilion (above). The Mustafa Paşa Pavilion.*

*The Mecidiye Pavilion.*

*The Constantine's Column (Çemberlitaş).*

*A panoramic view of the Beyazıt Square.*

the fourth courtyard where there are many pavilions in gardens. The only wooden pavilion in the complex, the Bagdat Pavilion, which is exquisitely decorated and tiled, as well as the Revan Pavilion, the Sünnet Pavilion and the Mecidiye Pavilion, which is the last building constructed in the palace complex, are found in this courtyard. The terrace in front of the Bagdat Pavilion commands a magnificent view of the Golden Horn, the Galata section of the city and old Istanbul with its skyline of domes and minarets.

## ÇEMBERLİTAŞ
## (The Constantine's Column)

It was erected to honour Constantine the Great, in the centre of an oval-shaped square on the second hill of Istanbul, and on the occasion of the dedication of Istanbul as the new capital of the Roman Empire in 330 A.D. The oval-shaped square, known as the Forum Constantine, was surrounded by columned porticos. Çemberlitaş is also known as the Hooped or Burnt Column. It stood taller than it does today, and a gilded statue of Constantine the Great, posing as the sun god, stood on it. The porphyry

blocks of the column, which had cracked in time and survived a fire, were reinforced with iron hoops.

The white marble capital was placed on it in the 12th century, and the stone wall seen in the lower section was built in the 18th century to reinforce the column. It was believed that relics dating back to early Christianity used to be kept in the small chamber under the column.

The course of the avenue that passes by the column has not changed since Constantine the Great.

## FORUM TAURI
## (Bayezid Square)

It was built in 393 during the reign of Theodosius I, as the largest square in the city. A gigantic victory arch used to stand in the middle of the square which was called the Bull's Square (Forum Tauri) because of the large bronze bull's head there.

There was a bronze statue of the emperor on the arch. Today, only a few marble blocks remain of the arch itself, but nothing remains of the monumental fountains which were to the north of the square. They used to be the largest fountains in the city then, and the Aqueducts of Valens used to supply

*The Gate of the University of Istanbul.*

*Used bookssellers market.*

*The Grand Bazaar (Kapalıçarşı).*

water to them. The buildings of the University of Istanbul occupy the large courtyard on the grounds where the Conqueror had built a palace. The monumental gate and the tallest tower in the city, the Bayezid fire-lookout tower, which stands in the gardens of the University, were built in the 19th century. The Bayezit Mosque and its complex (school and baths) are the main buildings around the square.

# THE COVERED BAZAAR
# (The Grand Bazaar)

The oldest and the largest covered market place in the world is situated in the centre of the city. Resembling a giant labyrinth, it consists of approximately sixty lanes and more than three-thousand shops. This unique and interesting market place is one of those places in the city which one must see to really appreciate.

In 1461, Mehmet the Conqueror built an area for the shops selling items necessary for the textile industry. This nucleus of today's Covered Bazaar (iç bedesten) is a rectangular area, surrounded inside and outside, by shops. The Conqueror built another area (sandal bedesteni) later, close to the "iç bedesten". There are shops only along the outer wall of the "sandal bedesten". During the time of the Conqueror, there were 950 shops.

The city-like bazaar is completely covered and it grew in size over the years. In the old days, each lane was reserved for a different profession and the quality of the handicrafts produced was strictly controlled. Business practices were governed by strict traditional ethics. Valuable fabrics, jewellery weapons and antique objets used to be sold by merchants whose families, for generations, had dealt in the same trade.

The bazaar, which was first built by the Conqueror and then enlarged by Süleiman the Magnificent, was originally constructed of wood. In 1700, it suffered greatly in a fire. In 1701, it was repaired by using stone and bricks, in the shape we see today.

The bazaar survived earthquakes, and a few fires towards the end of the last century. During repairs, it has lost its original form and features, and has changed for the worse.

Today, many of the streets in the bazaar have changed character. Guilds such as the "quilt makers", "slipper makers" and "fez makers" exist only in the street names.

*Different scenes from the Grand Bazaar (above).*  67  *A carpet store and a carpet repairer.*

Jewellers line the main street in the bazaar. The goldsmiths are on a side street at right angles to the main street. Prices vary, and bargaining is customary in these rather small stores. The Covered Bazaar still retains its old charm and is an attractive sight to see, but since 1970, modern and spacious shops have been built near the main entrance to shop in comfort. The bazaar is quite crowded at any hour of the day, and the shop owners try their best to attract the attention of shoppers and lure them into their shops. The spacious stores that line the street leading to the main entrance to the bazaar sell handmade items produced in Turkey.

## HANDMADE TURKISH CARPETS

The art of weaving hand-knotted carpets is the oldest handicraft of the Turks. The two richest carpet museums in the world are located in Istanbul. Today, carpets, still knotted in the old traditional ways, are produced in just about every region in Turkey. The carpets are made of pure wool, silk, or wool and cotton blends in various sizes and designs.

*A young girl weaving a carpet.*

*A "Carpet Show" in Bazaar 54 which has a rich carpet collection.*

Each carpet is a product of tradition, high quality raw materials, special techniques, patience and months long labour. Besides these, in certain centres, subsidized by the state, handmade carpets are produced like an industry.

Hereke, near Istanbul, is the most famous centre of handmade silk carpet production. The carpets made here, in Konya and in Kayseri are the most sought after carpets.

## SHOPPING IN ISTANBUL

The Grand Bazaar of Istanbul, with its thousands of shops is a famous and unique shopping centre. BAZAAR 54, the leading establishment in the Grand Bazaar, offers fully washed, top quality handmade carpets selected by experts. The old and new carpet collections of Bazaar 54, containing thousands of items of top quality Turkish workmanship, are Istanbul's largest and richest. Bazaar 54 is an authorized exporter with a worldwide shipping service. Besides carpets, its handmade, fully quaranteed jewellery collection is also worth seeing.

*A silk carpet from Hereke.*

*The Jewellery Section in Bazaar 54.*

69

*Bazaar 54 has a rich selection of Jewellery.*

*The interior of Süleymaniye Mosque.*

# THE SÜLEYMANİYE MOSQUE

Minarets and domes are the most attractive features of the skyline of Istanbul, and the largest and the most imposing mosque in the city is the Süleymaniye Mosque. The aesthetic supremacy of its interior and exterior, and its perfect proportions are fascinating. The Süleymaniye Mosque is an architectural masterpiece.

The 16th century was the golden age of the Ottoman Empire. Among the thirty-six sultans who ruled, Süleyman the Magnificent was the longest reigning sultan (47 years). This great sultan wanted to build a mosque honouring himself, and entrusted the construction to Sinan the Great, who is considered a genius in the world of architecture. He started the construction of the mosque and the complex surrounding it in 1550 and completed the project in 1557. Sinan initiated and developed the classical style in Turkish architecture. This mosque is a demonstration of his genius.

There were schools, a library, a public kitchen, a hospital, a caravanserai, baths and stores in the complex surrounding the courtyard of the main edifice. The beauty of the exterior of the mosque is best appreciated from a distance. The Galata Tower and the Galata district along the Golden Horn command a magnificent view of this imperial mosque. A huge dome covers the main chamber of the mosque with four minarets.

The entrance to the mosque is from an inner courtyard, surrounded by porticoes, and with an ablution fountain in the centre. The spaciousness, unity and exquisite decorations add to the imposing view of the interior. The 53 metre-high dome with a diameter of 26.50 metres, rests on four pillars. All the architectural elements in the interior are in perfect harmony. The static balance of the structure is perfect. Earthquakes that shake Istanbul have not caused even a single crack in the building. The interior of the dome was decorated with Baroque-influenced embellishments in the last century. The single piece, handmade carpet with mihrap design was spread on the floor in the 1960s.

The most attractive feature of the interior is the extraordinarily colourful, 16th century original stained glass windows with Turkish motifs in the wall of the mihrap. A very plain balcony for the chanters is situated next to the minber, and the marble wall of the mihrap niche is surrounded by deco-

rative tiles. The Imperial Pew is to the left of the mihrap. The interior walls are decorated with inscriptions of verses from the Koran, and these are some of the most beautiful examples of the Turkish art of calligraphy. The balconies reserved for women are along the side walls and the wall at the entrance. The brass grill partition seen on the south side of the interior is a beautiful example of 18th century Turkish metalwork, and it is a part of the library.

In the rear courtyard are the tombs of Süleyman the Magnificent and his beloved wife Roxelane. There are also the graves of important personalities. There is an inconspicuous, small grave in a corner of the complex. It is the plain grave of the great architect Sinan, who spent the fifty years of his ninety-nine years as the chief architect of the Ottoman Empire.

Sinan was a diligent and a productive architect who completed more than four-hundred pieces of work in his lifetime. He represents the school of Classic Turkish Architecture he founded. His apprentices, after him, created masterpieces in many Islamic lands.

## THE RÜSTEM PAŞA MOSQUE

This small mosque with a single minaret is situated on the Eminönü side of Galata Bridge, in the Hasırcılar Bazaar, near the Yeni Mosque and the Spice Bazaar. Eminönü is one of the busiest shopping districts in the city. Rising above the roofs of the office buildings surrounding it, this single-domed mosque together with the Süleymaniye Mosque, rising on the hill behind it, creates a beautiful sight. Sinan was commissioned by Grand Vizier Rüstem Paşa to build the mosque in 1561 on a terrace resting on a basement occupied by shops. A spiral staircase at each end gives access to the terrace. Its most interesting feature is its courtyard, which is designed as an extension of the portico at the entrance to the edifice and is covered by a roof. The portico is covered by five small domes resting on six columns.

The dome rises above the four wall pillars, opposite one another, and four columns, two on each side. There are four small semi-domes at each corner of the square chamber covered by a dome. There are galleries behind the columns on the sides. The facade where the entrance is, and the small but cosy

*The worshippers in the Süleymaniye Mosque.*

*The Süleymaniye Mosque at night (above).*

*Three different views of the Valide (Yeni) Mosque.*

*The Spice (Egyptian) Bazaar.*

*A store in the Spice Bazaar.*

and appealing interior are covered with the famous İznik tiles. The columns, the pillars, the mihrap and the walls of the galleries are all covered with tiles decorated with flower, leaf and geometric motifs. Therefore, the interior resembles a flower garden.

The coral-red colour was used only for a short period of time in the decoration of İznik tiles, in the second half of the 16th century. The colour appears like a relief on the tiles.

## THE VALİDE SULTAN MOSQUE (Yeni Cami)

It was the last imperial mosque built in the classical style. It was built next to the pier in Eminönü Harbour which was a very busy district then as well. Due to the heavy traffic on Galata Bridge and the heavy sea-traffic created by the boats docking at the piers in front of it, the mosque is seen by thousands of people every day.

Its construction was started by Safiye Sultan, mother of Sultan Mehmet III, in 1589, but it was interrupted in 1603 upon the death of the Sultan. Its architect was Davut Ağa, a student of Sinan. The construction was resumed in 1661 by Turhan Sultan, mother of the Sultan, and was completed in 1664.

Only the large covered bazaar, the mausoleums and the magnificent fountain of the mosque's scattered complex have survived.

Between the southern side of the mosque and the "L" shaped Spice Bazaar is the Flower Market. The tea houses here are always full of people resting. The Spice Bazaar is the second largest covered market place in the city.

The steamships, which had docked for fifty years in front of the mosque, have been taken out of service, and the minarets and the facades which had been blackened by soot have been cleaned.

## THE GOLDEN HORN (Haliç)

The Golden Horn, which is a natural harbour, played an important role in the development of the city of Istanbul. It is a narrow inlet separating the European side into two. Opposite the ancient city is the Galata district. The Golden Horn is approximately 8 km. long and its entrance from the Bosphorus is quite wide. Two streams drain into this inlet at its deeper end. There are no tides or currents in this unusually safe harbour which has been used since the establishment of the city. Due to the fertile

*The Galata Bridge: the first bridge over the Golden Horn.*

lands around it, the great variety of fish in its waters, the two streams draining into it and its shape, it was referred to as the Golden (meaning fertile) Horn. Throughout its history, a total of ten bridges were built on it. The first one was simple and built by Justinian. The Conqueror, also, built one during the seige of Istanbul. There were other bridges built for military purposes.

The oldest of the present three bridges is Galata Bridge built in 1836. The original bridge was made of wood. The one used today was completed in 1990.

During the Byzantine Empire, a thick chain used to be stretched across its entrance to keep enemy fleets out of the Golden Horn. Today, the vicinity of Galata Bridge, built at the entrance to the Golden Horn, is a site of heavy sea-traffic. Ferry boats serving the Islands and the districts along the Asian shores, and the big cruise ships that bring tourists use the docks in the area.

The shipyards and the Sepetçiler (Basket Weavers) Pavilion of the Topkapı Palace, the Sirkeci train station built in 1890, which is the last stop for trains arriving from Europe, the Valide Mosque and the Spice Bazaar line the shores at the entrance to the Golden Horn.

The Galata Bridge and its vicinity is the busiest and the most interesting part of the city. During all hours of the day, there is a heavy traffic of cars and pedestrians on the bridge which commands a magnificent view of the old city of Istanbul.

In the 1960s, many shipyards, factories, and other businesses were established along the shores of the Golden Horn, and they contributed to the pullution of its waters and the deterioration of the once scenic area. Since 1983, the pollution has been controlled and the area has started to recover. More than four-thousand houses, businesses and factories along its shores have been torn down and replaced by parks. With the completion of the new sewer system, the Golden Horn will again become a popular harbour for cruises. There is an interesting church on the shore of the historic city, after the Atatürk Bridge. Its mouldings and steel parts were made in Vienna and were brought here to be mounted on the building. It is called the Bulgarian Church. Further on is the Orthodox Patriarchate in the Fener district located amid the remains of the city walls and old districts. Across Fener, in the Kasımpaşa district, there is a big 19th century mansion which, today,

*A street lined with old houses, Eyüp.*

*Fener pier (above). Rowboats in the Golden Horn.*

houses the Navy Headquarters. The shipyards in Kasımpaşa, too, are being moved out of the Golden Horn. The Aynalı Kavak Pavilion, too, is located in this district.

## THE EYÜP SULTAN MOSQUE

The Eyüp Mosque, its mausoleum and its complex are located outside the historic city, to the north of the corner where the city walls along the Golden Horn meet the land walls. Since the Eyüp district is situated on the shore, on the land side of the third bridge accross the Golden Horn where it starts to taper, it can be reached by ferry boats too.

Eyüp is considered a sacred site by Moslems. Eyüp-el-Ensari, the flag bearer of Mohammed, was killed here in the 7th century during the Arab seige. His grave, discovered during the conquest of Istanbul, was enclosed by a large mausoleum, and next to it the first prominent mosque in Istanbul was built. The original mosque, built by the Conqueror, collapsed in an earthquake in the 18th century and was replaced by another mosque, completed in 1800. On holy days of Islam and every Friday, the mausoleum of Eyüp is visited by throngs of believers. The cen-

*The Eyüp Sultan Mosque.*

turies-old trees, flocks of pigeons flying and believers praying create a lively and mystic atmosphere in the environs of the mosque and the mausoleums.

The exterior walls of the mausoleum facing the mosque's courtyard are decorated with tiles from different periods. Historical sources indicate that even during the Byzantine era, Eyüp was a prominent village where the existence of the grave of a holy person was known, and during times of drought, prayers for rain used to be organized here.

After the Conqueror, each succeeding sultan concluded his coronation and sword- bearing ceremonies by visiting the Eyüp Sultan district. Cemeteries occupy the lands on the hills and slopes behind the district.

The famous Pierre Loti Café is on the first hill behind the Eyüb district. The famous poet-author Pierre Loti, who loved Istanbul, came here quite often to admire the view of the Golden Horn. During the full moon, the view of the Golden Horn, as seen from this cosy little house and the terrace in front of it, leaves long lasting impression on the visitor.

*The Piyerloti Café.*

# THE KARİYE MUSEUM
## (The Church of St. Saviour in Chora Monastery)

The word chora means "outside the city, the countryside". Probably, a small church which had been built here before the 5th century Roman city walls gave its name to the other churches built later at the same site. The existing edifice is dated to the 11th-14th centuries. Besides its attractive exterior, the mosaics and frescoes inside are masterpieces of "the Renaissance" of Byzantine art. These decorations and the additions built in the 14th century were made upon the orders of Theodore Metochites.

The mosaic panels seen in the two narthexes upon entering depict scenes from the lives of the Virgin and Christ (as described in the Bible). Frescoes depicting religious themes are in the side chapel. Figures of the members of the palace and the church are seen among them. When the church was converted into a mosque in the beginning of the 16th century, the mosaics and frescoes were covered by

*The Kariye (Chora) Museum.*

*Emperor Theodorus presenting the model of Chora to Christ.*

*Three different views of the interior of the Kariye Museum.*

*Jesus saving the souls of Adam and Eve, a frescoe (above). The Presentation of Mary to Bishop Zacharias (below).*

whitewash. Starting in 1950, these have been restored and cleaned by the Byzantine Institute of the U.S.A.

The Chora monastery and its church became neighbours with the imperial palaces and acquired importance in time. Master craftsmen decorated the building with great care under the difficult conditions present in the 14th century.

The famous scholar and state dignitary of the time, Theodore Metochites, built the side chapel, which was completed in 1320, and the exonarthex. The mosaics and frescoes were also completed during his time. The mosaic panels were created by a group of artisans. The mosaics of the upper sections of the nave have not survived.

In Byzantine art, the name or the monogram of the personality depicted used to be inscribed next to the figure.

The vicinity of Kariye Museum, which resembles a picture gallery, has been changed in recent times. The old houses have been restored and turned into cafés and pension houses.

*The geneology of Christ (detail).*

*Dormition of the Virgin Mary.*

82

*The City Walls in Topkapı.*

*The Tekfur Palace.*

## THE TEKFUR PALACE

Roman and early Byzantine palaces used to be situated near the Hippodrome. The Blachernae Palace, where the Byzantine emperors lived, (probably from the 7th or 8th centuries until the conquest), was spread over a wide area where the city walls reached the Golden Horn. The only surviving pavilion of this palace complex is the Tekfur Palace and it was built adjacent to the city walls

The three-storeyed pavilion (its roof is missing) was built in the 12th century. It has a small courtyard and its ornate facade is decorated with rows of brick and stone. Rows of arches and supports decorate the windows. The ground storey of the pavilion has access to the Thedosius City Walls. In the 18th century, the palace was used as a workshop where tiles were produced.

## THE CITY WALLS

The historic city of Istanbul is located on a triangular peninsula which is surrounded by city walls on three sides. The walls seen today were built during the Roman era and extend a total of 22 kms.

*The interior of Yedikule Museum.*

After the establishment of Byzantion, the city was enlarged four times, and each time the city walls were built more towards the west.

Because of its geographical location, the peninsula can be easily defended. Not so rugged terrain extending from the Balkans end at the colossal city walls on the landward side of the city. There were sturdy city walls along the shores of the Golden Horn and the Sea of Marmara, too.

Nothing has remained from the first walls built around the acropolis of Byzantion, the second walls built in the beginning of the 3rd century by emperor Septimius Severius, or the third walls built in the 320s by Constantine the Great.

The most important section of city walls was the one in the west, on the landward side. This extraordinarily strong wall stretched from the sea to the Golden Horn and was built over three different periods. There are many inscriptions pertaining to the restoration of the city walls during the late Byzantine and Turkish eras.

The city gate, which is also the entrance to the palace section, was built in the 7th and 8th centuries. On the gate, there is a tower known as the Anamas Tower. The land walls measure 6,492 metres in length from the sea to the Golden Horn. In recent years, the land around the walls have been cleared of debris and many parks have been built. Sections of the walls which have been damaged in earthquakes and in time have been repaired.

The most magnificent gate was the Golden Gate (Altın Kapı) near the Sea of Marmara. This imperial gate was placed like a victory arch between the two protruding marble towers. Victorious armies and emperors entered through the Golden Gate.

## YEDİKULE (The Seven Towers)

The first Turkish-built complex after the conquest of Istanbul, consisted of five towers with walls between them. It surrounded the Golden Gate, turning it into an inner fortress. This section of the city walls with five towers, surrounding the Golden Gate, created the concept of an inner fortress in Turkish city-planning.

Originally, Yedikule used to house the treasury. Later it was used as a prison where certain ambassadors were imprisoned. Today, Yedikule, with its interesting looking entrance, the Golden Gate and its towers, is a museum.

*The Galata Tower.*

*A Turkish belly dancer.*

## GALATA AND GALATA TOWER

The Galata district is situated in an area that commands a view of the entrance to the Golden Horn and the harbour. During the Byzantine and Ottoman eras, the district was settled first by the Venetians and then, beginning in the 14th century, by the Genoese. Latin merchants used to control commerce in the Galata district where, in the 14th and 15th centuries, a tall lookout-tower and city walls were built. Many of the streets in the district are lined with eighty and ninety year old houses, and Galata resembles the cities along the Mediterranean coast in that age. For many years, people who came to Istanbul from different parts of Anatolia settled in this district. Many of the churches and synagogues in the area are still serving today, along with the German, French, Austrian and Greek schools. The Arap Mosque, here, has an interesting architectural style and it is one of the important religious monuments in the district.

The tower was built in the 14th century, on the hill in the district with the same name, as the main tower of the Galata city walls. Located at a site overlooking the harbour and the entrance to the Bosphor-

us, it commands a magnificent view of the historic city. The upper sections of the tower were constructed in the Turkish era when it was used as a fire-watch tower. Its conical cap was restored to its original, early 19th century form in 1969. A restaurant and a night club occupy the upper two storeys, and a balcony surrounds the tower.

## TÜNEL (the subway) AND BEYOĞLU

The entrance to the Tünel (the subway), which connects the shores of the Golden Horn to the Beyoğlu district on the hill, is located in the Karaköy Square. One of the first three subways in Europe, it was opened for services in 1880, and today, it is the shortest subway in the world.

İstiklal Caddesi stretches on the hills in the Beyoğlu district which starts at the upper entrance to "Tünel", and extends all the way to the Taksim Square. Beginning in 16th century, Beyoğlu became the district where foreign embassy buildings were constructed and minorities settled. Near the upper entrance to Tünel is the Galata Mevlevihanesi (lodge) which is the Divan Edebiyatı (old Ottoman Poetry) Museum today. There are interesting collec-

*Atatürk's statue in the Taksim Square.*

*The İstiklal Avenue, Beyoğlu.*

tions of books and musical instruments.

Istiklal Caddesi is the main street famous for its elegant shops, lively nightlife, theatres and cinemas. Except for the nostalgic street car, the street is closed to traffic. The Catholic churches seen on the side of the street overlooking the Bosphorus have been in service since the last century.

Halfway towards Taksim Square is the small Galatasaray Square where the famous school with the same name is located. Across the school there is a partially collapsed buildings known as the Flower Passage, where there are many small restaurants and beerhouses. The street running next to this passage is lined with shops selling varieties of fish, vegetables and fruit.

# TAKSİM

The Taksim Square, with the statue of Atatürk in the center, is surrounded by the Atatürk Cultural Centre in the north and five star hotels, and it is considered the centre of modern day Istanbul.

Cumhuriyet Caddesi stretches from the square to the Şişli district, and there are many travel agencies along this road. After the Radio House, the Officers Club and Guest House, and the Military Museum, come the shops and boutiques selling high quality clothing, shoes etc.

## THE MILITARY MUSEM

Considered the second largest military museum in the world, the Military Museum and Culture Center has been moved to its new quarters in Harbiye, and opened to the public on February 10, 1993. In the 19.000 m$^2$ area only nine-thousand of the fiftytwo-thousand items are exhibited in twentytwo halls. The items are displayed under the following catagories: Shooting Weapons, Cavalry, Yavuz Sultan Selim, Fatih Sultan Mehmet (the Conqueror) Cutting Weapons, Early Islamic Swords, Persian Swords, Caucasian Swords, Turkish Weapons, Blades, European Cutting Weapons, Defense Weapons, Armours, Fire Weapons, Mahmut Şevket Paşa, Ethnographic Items, Tents, Banners, Military Uniforms. The most important items on exhibit are the banner used in the Kosova Battle, the helmet of Orhan Gazi, a 17th century Imperial tent, the chain the Byzantines stretched across the Golden Horn and the swords of the Conqueror and Yavuz Sultan Selim.

*A costume of Yeniçeri.*

## THE JANISSARY BAND

The official band of the Ottoman-Turkish army was known as the Mehter (the Janissary Band). This band of thousands of members used to lead the armies going on campaigns. The band, which had its own special way of marching, used to play encouraging marches during wars and seiges. Today, the band still plays the oldest military music in the world, by using the old, original musical instruments, on certain days in the Military Museum, and during special ceremonies and concerts.

## THE BOSPHORUS

One of the most beautiful places in the world is the Bosphorus, which is a strait that runs a winding course between the two continents from one sea to the other. It is a natural border between Europe and Asia, and it is the only outlet of the Black Sea. The Black Sea is connected to the Aegean through the Bosphorus and the Dardanelles.

With the old seaside mansions, mosques, palaces, restaurants and beaches along its shores, the Bosphorus resembles a wide river. Woods and residences cover the hills rising behind its shores. It looks

*Two different views of the Bosphorus Bridge.*

89

*The Fatih Sultan Mehmet Bridge.*

*A view of the Bosphorus.*

magnificent in each season and is especially beautiful in the spring when it is adorned with the pink flowers of Judas trees. The Bosphorus is unforgettable.

The two fortresses on opposite shores, constructed halfway up the Bosphorus, stand facing each other. These were built by the Turks. These and the other fortresses, on the hills near the Black Sea, built in earlier times, are the military installations indicating the strategic importance of the Bosphorus in every age. When viewed from the Sea of Marmara end, from where the historic city looks most impressive, the Bosphorus appears like a small bay. The rest of the 30 kilometre- long stretch, up to the Black Sea, appears as consecutive lakes. The first suspension bridge across the Bosphorus was completed in 1973 and the second one in 1988. Only an aerial- view shows that the Bosphorus is actually a strait.

The Bosphorus is a unique "sea-river". The less saline waters of the Black Sea flow towards the Sea of Marmara on the surface, while below the surface, there is another current flowing in the opposite direction. Due to these strong surface currents and lack of roads, there were few settlements along its shores up until the end of the last century. In the 19th century, besides the small villages, imperial palaces and the summer residences of the wealthy and of the foreign embassies started to appear along its shores. Development of the shores of the Bosphorus began upon the initiation of ferry services by the Hayriye Corporation (Şirket-i Hayriye) which was founded in 1852. It was the first corporation founded in the Ottoman state. Today, the residential districts along its shores are served by modern roads, suspension bridges and ferry boats, and are included within the borders of the metropolis. The strait, which was a river valley in the Ice Age, has a rich marine fauna. It has an average depth of 50 metres and a maximum depth of 112 metres. Different kinds of fish are caught along its shores as well as in the seas nearby. Different species of fish migrate through these waters seasonally.

The name "Bosphorus" is derived from a story in mythology and it means the "Bull's Passage". Since it is an easily traversed passage, it facilitated the development of trade and other relations between the civilizations in Asia and Europe.

*A seaside mansion along the Bosphorus.*

*The Beşiktaş pier.*

The Bosphorus, its extension, the Golden Horn, and the peninsula on which the historic city of Istanbul developed have been the most sought after locations in the world during the last 2,500 years. Many military expeditions, and migrations between Asia and Europe used this passage. The campaign of the Argonauts to the Black Sea is the first mythological story about the Bosphorus. In the 6th century B.C. the Persian armies, in order to cross the Bosphorus easily, tied their boats together side by side, thus forming the first bridge on the Bosphorus.

## THE LEANDER'S TOWER

Western sources erroneously state that this is the spot where Leander drowned as he was trying to swim across the strait to be with his lover, Hera. Actually, this incident took place in the Dardanelles, not in the Bosphorus.

This rather small structure known, as the Maiden's Tower (Kız Kulesi), stands on a small islet and has become one of the symbols of Istanbul. Through the ages, it was used as a watchtower and a lighthouse. Today, it serves as a landmark for ships en-

*The Leander's Tower at sunset.*

*A panoramic view from Üsküdar (the seashore).*

tering the Bosphorus, and has not been changed since the last century.

## ÜSKÜDAR

The district across the Leander's Tower is an old settlement called Üsküdar. The shortest route connecting Europe to Asia used to pass through here. The 16th century mosques the monumental fountain, as well as the small Şemsi Paşa Mosque and its schools built by Sinan on the seashore are fine examples of Turkish art.

## KADIKÖY

The Kadıköy district, along the shores of the Sea of Marmara, does not possess any historic buildings. It was one of the fastest growing districts in Istanbul during the last twenty years. It is located at the site of the ancient village of Chalcedon where there were many monasteries and where, in the 5th century A.D., the Ecumenical Council met several times. Only a few of the 19th and 20 th century mansions, and houses in gardens by the seashore and inland have survived. Yachting clubs, harbours, beaches

*The Kadıköy pier.*

93

and wide roads line the seashore in Kadıköy. The famous Bağdad Caddesi (Baghdad Avenue) is the shopping area. Fenerbahçe, a headland, is an ideal picnic area and a promenade.

Haydarpaşa Railway Station, built in 1906 in Prussian architectural style, was the first railway station of the Bagdat Railways in Asia and it is located between Kadıköy and Üsküdar. Cemeteries for the English and French soldiers who lost their lives in the Crimean War occupy the slopes near the station.

There are two huge buildings behind the modern port facilities. The one with clocktowers is a university, and the one next to it, with four big towers, is the Selimiye Barracks, built in early 19th century. Florence Nightingale served here as a nurse, and her room in the barracks, a section of which was used as a hospital during the Crimean War, is still kept in its original condition.

The slopes behind Üsküdar are occupied by the historic Karacaahmet Cemetery. A little further inland are Büyük and Küçük Çamlıca hills. These hills, covered with woods, command a magnificent aerial view of the Princes'Islands, the Bosphorus,

*The Ortaköy Mosque.*

*Ortaköy and the Bosphorus Bridge in the winter.*

the old city and the suspension bridges.

An elegant café, built and run by the Turkish Touring Club, is located on top of the Büyük Çamlıca hill.

## CRUISES ON THE BOSPHORUS

Scheduled ferry boats that leave from Eminönü and near the Dolmabahçe Palace, cruise boats, owned by some of the hotels and tour agencies, as well as privately owned and operated smaller boats are the best vehicles to use for a cruise on the Bosphorus. These cruises run a zigzag course up the Bosphorus towards the Black Sea with Asia on the right and Europe on the left. The Leander's Tower is at the entrance to the Bosphorus and The Dolmabahçe Palace is on the shore opposite Üsküdar. Five star hotels rise on the hills behind the shores. The Çırağan Palace Hotel, along with the Bosphorus Bridge, is seen a little further up. The 1,074 metre-long section of the suspension bridge extends between the continents.

The Ortaköy Mosque is next to the foot of the bridge on the European side, and Beylerbeyi Palace

*An old seaside mansion along the Bosphorus.*

*A passanger rowboat in the Bosphorus (18th century).*

*Fishermen along the shores of Bosphorus in the Kuleli district.*

is next to the foot of the bridge on the Asian side. Therefore, one gets a chance to see both contemporary and old monuments side by side. Villa Bosphorus, (near Beylerbeyi Palace), where the tours on the Asian shores and the cruises on the Bosphorus stop for a brief rest and shopping, commands a splendid view of Bosphorus Bridge.

Old seaside mansions next to modern residences line both shores of the Bosphorus, and hills adorned with different tones of green rise behind them.

The wide, yellow building with two towers, seen after the first bridge, on the Asian shore going towards the Black Sea, is the famous Kuleli Military Academy (19th century). In the Bebek district, on the opposite shore, is a large, interesting looking building which houses the Egyptian Consulate. The Bay of Bebek is a natural yacht harbour, and the 20th century mosque on the seashore is a small structure in classic Turkish architectural style.

## THE DOLMABAHÇE PALACE

The Dolmabahçe Palace, a blend of many European architectural styles, was built between 1843 and 1856 by Karabet Balyan, the chief architect of Sultan Abdülmecit. Ottoman Sultans owned many palaces and pavilions but Topkapı Palace was the official residence. Yet, after its completion, the Dolmabahçe Palace was abandoned.

The three-storeyed palace, built on a symmetrical plan, has 285 rooms and 43 halls. There is a 600 metre-long quay along the sea, and there are two monumental gates, one of which is very ornate, on the land side. In the middle of the palace, surrounded by well-kept gardens, is a large, elevated hall used for meetings and balls. The wing near the entrance was used for the Sultans' receptions and meetings; and the wing on the other side of the ballroom was the Harem. The palace has survived intact with its original decorations, furniture, silk carpets, curtains and everything else. The magnificent palace is full of unique, extremely valuable objects. Its walls and ceilings are covered with paintings by the famous artists of the age and with decorations made by using tons of gold. All the furnishings in the main rooms and halls are in different tones of the same colour. Very ornate wood parquet, different in each room, covers the floors. Famous silk and wool carpets of Hereke, some of the finest examples of the Turkish art of carpet weaving, cover the floors.

*The Dolmabahçe Palace as seen from the sea.*

Rare handmade object d'art from Europe and the Far East decorate every room in the palace. Brilliant crystal chandeliers, candelabras and fireplaces add to the lavish decor.

Of the six baths in the palace, the one used by the Sultan is made of unusually richlooking, specially carved alabaster marble.

The ballroom is the largest of its kind in the world. A 4.5 ton giant-sized chandelier hangs from the 36 metre-high dome. The hall, which is used for important political meetings, balls and signing of treaties, used to be heated by a heating system under the floor until electricity and central heating were installed later. The upper galleries of the hall were reserved for orchestras and the diplomatic corps.

Long hallways lead to the Harem section of the palace where the bedrooms of the Sultan and the quarters of his mother, the quarters of the ladies of the Harem and the servants were located. The hallways leading to the Harem have many consecutive doors. More than six-hundred valuable paintings in the palace hang on the walls in the hallways.

The fourth addition to the palace is as large as the Harem and it was used as the quarters of the Crown Prince. The entrance to this section is from outside the palace complex, and today, it houses the

*The northern gate of the Dolmabahçe Palace.*

Museum of Fine Arts.

Atatürk, founder of the Republic of Turkey, used to stay in this palace during his stays in Istanbul. When he died here in 1938, before his body was taken to Ankara, he laid in state in the palace so that his people could have a chance to pay their last respects to him. All the clocks in the palace were stopped at 9:05 a.m., the time of his death, in memory of this great Turk.

The palace which is a museum today is open on certain days of the week, and it is one of those historic places in Istanbul that must be seen. There are collections of precious objects used by the sultans and members of the palace in everyday life and during ceremonies. Some of these have been taken out of storage and are being displayed in two different rooms. Most of these gold, silver and crystal objects, teasets and table settings, dresser sets and other decorative objects are of European origin, and each one is a very valuable piece of art.

The rear gardens of the palace and the aviary, along with some of the mansions here, have been renovated and opened to the public. Most recently,

*The Dolmabahçe Palace: the Muayede Hall.*

*An oil painting in the Naval Museum: The war of Lepanto (1571).*

the Concubines' Quarters was opened to the public. The aviary section has a separate entrance from the main street. The long entrance hall is used as a picture gallery today. The garden reached through here is the section behind the ballroom. The aviary has been renovated and today, there are many big cages with colourful exotic birds.

The two side by side pavilions are known as the H areket Pavilions, and used for exhibitions and other cultural events.They are reached through the entrance to the Fine Arts Museum in Beşiktaş.

The monumental watchtower, located next to the entrance used today, was built by Sultan Abdülhamit II between 1890-1895 and it still operates, today.

## THE MUSEUM OF FINE ARTS, TURKISH PAINTING AND SCULPTURES

It occupies the fourth section, the quarters of the Crown Prince, in the Dolmabahçe Palace. The entrance to the museum and the Hareket Pavilion, which is used for special exhibits, is on the seaward side of Beşiktaş.

This section of the palace consists of three storeys of rooms and large halls. The first floor is reserved for various exhibitions, and the upper storey for the works of art in the museum. Restoration of the upper sections and the facade of the building has been completed, and that of the interior is being carried out a section at a time.

Works of Turkish painters from the 19th century upto today are found in the museum. There are approximately 2,500 original paintings, 250 reproductions and 400 statues in the museums which will soon be modernized. Contemporary Turkish works of art are displayed from time to time in the special sections in the museums and palaces in Istanbul, in the Atatürk Cultural Centre and in certain other art galleries.

## THE NAVAL MUSEUM

Situated in the Beşiktaş district along the shores of the Bosphorus, this museum is next to the park where the statue and the mausoleum of the famous 16th century Turkish Admiral Barbaros Hayreddin are located. Old boats are displayed in the main

*A view of the exterior of the Yıldız Palace.*

building, and along with the interesting items in the gardens, the museum has an impressive collection. The main building is three-storeyed, and models of boats, sections from Atatürk's personal yacht, tools and other items used in the decoration of old ships are displayed in the small rooms and halls of the building. Paintings depicting various naval events decorate the walls. Weapons used in different periods cannons and important banners are on display on the top floor. Naval uniforms are displayed on dummies. The basement is reserved for the parts and sections of the ships which had served in the Turkish navy. There are also torpedoes on display. Behind the main building, there is another buildings entered from the sea side. It is reserved for the Old Boats Gallery. The well preserved, elegant boats of the Sultans, members of the palace and other important people of the 18th-20th centuries are displayed. Sail boats, row boats, replicas, parts of ships and other mementoes are displayed in the large halls.

## THE YILDIZ PALACE

The gardens of the palace and the pavilions are open to the public. The Şale Pavilion is a palace mu-

*The Malta Pavilion of the Yıldız Palace Complex.*

*A view of the interior of the Yıldız Palace.*

seum and the other sections of the palace are either closed or used for other purposes.

The fashion of building palace complexes made of small pavilions was abandoned in the 19th century after the completion of the Yıldız Palace complex. The complex which grew over the years, is located in an area of hills and valleys, and it is surrounded by high walls. The palace complex was connected to the Çırağan Palace by a bridge, and it commands a fabulous view of the Bosphorus.

The Yıldız Palace spreads over a very large piece of land, just like the classic Turkish palaces i.e. the Topkapı Palace, and it consists of many mansions, pavilions and other buildings in courtyards with gardens. The complex covers an area of approximately 500,000 m$^2$ and it is the second largest palace complex in the city.

The first pavilion was constructed in the beginning of the 19th century in the hunting area. Many others were built until the beginning of the 20th century. The palace gained importance during the reign of Sultan Abdülhamid II, in the late 19th century. Sultan Abdülhamid, who was a very suspicious person, felt secure in this palace and did not use the others during his thirty- three year reign. With the

military barracks outside and the other establishments inside the complex, he created a city-like complex for himself.

The palace grounds is surrounded by very tall walls, and there are other walls on the palace grounds separating it into courtyards with gardens. These courtyards are connected to each other by passageways and have pavilions, pools, greenhouses, workshops, aviaries and other minor buildings. There are two main entrances to the palace grounds and there is a mosque next to each one. A large section of the grounds has been turned into a public park and it is called the Yıldız Park. The Malta and Çadır (Tent) Pavilions have been renovated by the Turkish Touring Club and today, they serve as cafés run by the same club.

Workshops, producing porcelainware, built in this section of the complex are still producing the best hand- made porcelain and tiles of the Turkish art of pottery.

Until recently, the reception hall used by the sultans, the Harem and the other buildings in the vicinity were housing the military academy. Therefore, they are devoid of their original decorations and furniture, and today house the different departments of

*The Çırağan Palace which has been restored and turned into a hotel.*

certain universities and organizations. The extensions of these buildings, like the armoury, the officers' quarters, the theatre and the garden with a pool have been renovated and are used for exhibitions, concerts and other social functions.

## THE ÇIRAĞAN PALACE

The best locations along the Bosphorus and the Golden Horn were reserved for the palaces and mansions of the sultans or important personalities. Many of these, however, have disappeared in time. One of those, the Çırağan Seaside Palace, burned down in 1910.

The palace, which had been constructed at the site of an old wooden mansion by Sultan Abdülaziz, was completed in 1871. Its architect was Serkis Balyan, the palace architect. The construction took four years and cost four million gold pieces. The ceilings used to be covered with exquisite woodwork and its walls, with marble. Its colums were masterpieces of stone works and the rooms were lavishly furnished. Mother-of-pearl inlaid and gold gilded furniture and exquisite carpets filled the rooms. Just like the other palaces decorating the shores of the Bosphorous, it

had witnessed many of the important events of the last century. Its exterior was made of colourful marble and it was connected to the Yıldız Palace on the slopes behind it. High walls on the landward side separated it from the road. The gates of the palace are imposing.

The extension of the palace on the city-side has been restored and is used as the State's Guest House.

The palace has been restored and with the addition of new buildings, it has been turned into a five-star hotel.

## THE BEYLERBEYİ PALACE

Situated near the foot of the Bosphorus Bridge on the Asian shore, this was a seaside imperial mansion used during the summer the Since. Byzantine period, Beylerbeyi district has been a summer resort where there are many imperial mansions and gardens. The palace was built at the site of a wooden mansion between the years 1861-1865 by Sultan Abdulmecit. Western motifs along with Turkish and eastern motifs were used to decorate the building. It has two sections: the Harem (for ladies) and the Selamlık (for men). Including the ground floor, the

*The Beylerbeyi Palace as seen from the sea (above).*

*A view of the interior of the Beylerbeyi Palace.*

*Villa Bosphorus in Beylerbeyi, a distinguished shopping center on the Asian shore.*

*The Rumeli Fortress.*

mansion is three- storeyed and has twenty-six rooms and six halls. The small pavilions located at each end of the long quay were for recreation. There are gardens and terraces with pools behind the building. The Stable Pavilion here is the finest example of its kind, and the pavilions nearby were built before it.

The large mansion has a well-arranged garden and a richly ornamented marble exterior.

The large hall in the centre section of the palace has a pool, and a spiral staircase. This striking area displays different artistic styles. During its golden days, the mansion was used during the summers, and also to accommodate visiting state dignitaries. It has been preserved in its original condition.

Near the imperial seaside mansion is the Villa Bosphorus which offers an excellent opportunity to rest and shop, during the tours to the Asiatic shores of the Bosphorus or during a boat ride.

This famous shopping center. Occupies the gardens of an old seaside mansion and the street near by. In the section located in the gardens is the Villa Bosphorus where fabolous jewellery is sold. The Sultan Deri store where leather goods are sold and the Asiatic Bazaar where souvenirs are sold are located on the street section.

*The Küçüksu Pavilion.*

*The Anatolian Fortress.*

## (The European Fortress)
## RUMELİ HİSARI

The city had been beseiged many times before the final seige of Istanbul by the Conqueror in 1453, but had managed to defend itself with the help of the Roman city walls. Even during long seiges, provisions were managed to be brought into the city via the sea. Therefore, to prevent any reinforcements and help coming from the Black Sea during the seige, before the final seige started, a fortress was built on the European shore, opposite the other Turkish fortress built earlier on the Asian shore. The fortress was completed in an amazingly short time of four months in 1452. This largest and strongest fortress of the Middle Ages lost its strategic importance right after the fall of the city. A fine example of classic Turkish fortress architecture, this impressive fortress is another element adorning the Bosphorus. It was restored in the 1950s and turned into a museum. During the annual Festival of Arts, the gardens of the fortress is used as an amphitheatre.

Between the compus and the European Fortress is the area called Aşian. The house of famous Turkish poet Tevfik Fikret, localed in this area and also called the Aşian, has been turned into a museum.

## THE KÜÇÜKSU PAVILION

This seaside mansion in a big garden is located on the Asian shore, by the Küçüksu Park between the two streams draining into the Bosphorus. The first mansion was built by Sultan Mahmut I in 1751 under the supervision of Grand Vizier Divittar Mehmet Pasha. It was renovated by Sultan Selim III (1792) and by Sultan Mahmut II. In 1856, the mansion we see today was built by Sultan Abdülmecit. The three-storeyed building, including the ground storey, is in Rococco and Baroque styles. In each storey, there is a main hall surrounded by four rooms. The mansion was built to house very brief stays. It is also called Göksu Mansion. Its furnishings are original. Near the mansion, there is a public fountain built in 1806 for Sultan Mustafa III's wife, Sultan Mihrişah.

*The Göksu  stream in Anadolu Hisarı (above).*

*The Emirgan Minucipal  Park and  the Sarı Mansion.*

*The Tarabya Bay and the Grand Tarabya Hotel.*

## (The Anatolian Fortress)
## ANADOLU HİSARI

The fortress is situated by the Küçüksu Park and on the shore of the Göksu stream on the Asian side. It is quite a small fortress built between 1390 and 1391, before the European Fortress on the opposite shore, by Sultan Bayezid, to control the traffic on the Bosphorus and as a step in the preparations for the final seige of Istanbul. A street passes through this picturesque fortress, situated at a strategic location by the sea, next to the stream that drains into the Bosphorus. There are old wooden houses resting against the small towers of the fortress.

The Kanlıca district, which comes after the fortress, is famous for its yoghurt and seaside cafés. The Asian tower of the new "Fatih Bridge" is situated here, too.

## EMİRGÂN AND TARABYA

The Emirgan district, along the European coast of the Bosphorus, attracts attention by its greenery and quaint appearance. During the weekends, people like to sit under the old oak trees and sip tea. Along

*The Tarabya Bay.*

*Shores of the Sarıyer district.*

*The Sadberk Hanım Museum, Post-delivery Resting Room.*

the shore, an old ottoman seaside mansion called the Şerifler Mansion attracts the attention. The woods covering the hills and the slopes make up the Emirgân Municipal Park where there are many lanes for strolling, and three mansions serving as tea houses. The annual Tulip Festival is held here each spring.

Below the park is the small Bay of Istinye which, for many years, housed the shipyards. These shipyards have been moved to another area and the natural beauty of the bay has been restored.

A branch of the road that stretches from the city center towards the Bosphorus over the hills joins the shore at the Bay of Tarabya, which is a small yacht harbour. On one side of the harbour is the summer residence of the German Embassy and a beach, and on the other side, the five-star Tarabya Hotel. Restaurants serving fish dishes and Turkish appetizers surround the harbour.

## SARIYER

Summer residences of foreign embassies, restaurants, cafés, seaside mansións and restaurants line the street that extends along the shore upto the

Sarıyer district from where the Black Sea end of the Bosphorus is seen. The road that separates from the street in Sarıyer leads to the Belgrade Forest, which starts on the slopes behind the Büyükdere district, and then continues to the Kilyos Beach on the coast of the Black Sea.

The last residential district after Sarıyer, along the Bosphorus on the European side, is the Rumeli Kavağı district which is the last stop for the ferries operating on the Bosphorus. Rumeli Kavağı is a small fishing village famous for its fish restaurants. Rumeli Feneri (lighthouse) is the last district on the European coast of the Bosphorus.

## THE SADBERK HANIM MUSEUM

It is an interesting museum founded by the Vehbi Koç Family Foundation. It occupies a three-storeyed wooden house in an interesting European style. Located in the Sarıyer district, along the shores of the Bosphorus near the Black Sea, the museum was founded to exhibit the rare objects collected by the Koç family over the years. There are shops and a

*The Sadberk Hanım Museum, a Kütahya water pitcher.*

*The Sadberk Hanım Museum, a Kütahya water cup.*

*Şile and the wide beaches in Şile.*

rest area on the ground floor and gardens in the back.

The collections are exhibited in the rooms and halls in the upper storeys. The collections, especially the items used in 19th century everyday life are exhibited in showcases. These objects are very valuable from the ethnographical point of view. There are sections where scenes from the everyday life of one or two generations ago, including the clothes worn then, decorations and other items characteristic of the age are displayed on dummies. There are also samples of valuable fabrics, as well as gold, porcelain and silver objects.

The addition of Hüseyin Kocabaş Collection to the museum enriched the Roman, Byzantine, Seljouk and Ottoman collections.

## KİLYOS

This small village on the Black Sea coast, on the European side, is famous for its wide, sandy beaches. Roads running either through the Belgrade Forests or over the hills behind Sarıyer lead to Kilyos. The reservoirs and aqueducts that supply water to Istanbul are scattered in the forest. The beaches in Kilyos, which is only 25 kms. from the center Istanbul, are very popular. Accommodations in the village include a motel and pension houses.

## ŞİLE

Şile is a lovely little fishing town near İstanbul. It is located on the Anatolian side of the Black Sea coast, 65 kms from Üsküdar, and a winding road through woods leads to the famous, wide beaches.

The view of the small harbour with a lighthouse is worth seeing. Next to the harbour is the remains of a Genoese tower. Endless beaches extend towards the west and numerous small coves are seen in the east.

There are many hotels and pension houses in this charming town.

## THE PRINCES' ISLANDS

The archipelago known as the Princes' Islands consists of nine various sized islands in the Sea of Marmara and is only an hour away by boat from the pier in the Golden Horn. During the Byzantine era there were many monasteries some of which were

used as imperial summer residences and some to house the exiled.

Heybeli Ada is the second largest islands in the archipelago. A small church (the last Byzantine structure built before the fall of Byzantium) dedicated to the Virgin is situated in the inner courtyard of the Naval Academy on the island. There are also unidentified ruins in other parts of the island. In the beginning of the 19th century, when steamboats started serving the islands, the population of the islands began to increase.

The four larger islands are popular summer resorts with ideal picnic areas and beautiful beaches. The islands are heavily populated from May until the end of September, and then become almost desolate in winter. Scheduled ferry boats serve the islands from the mainland. Throughout the summer and especially on weekends, private boats, yachts and sail-boats anchor in the beautiful coves around every island.

Motor vehicles are not allowed on the islands, the shores of which are lined by the summer residences of the wealthy, beaches and picnic areas. Horse-drawn carriages are the only means of transportation.

*A Horse-drawn carriages in Büyükada.*

*Merit Halki Palace Hotel: Located on the second largest Prince Island Heybeliada, this historical building has been renovated in 1994. Surrounded by pine tress, the Hotel offers all the services of a 4 star Hotel.*

*Hotel Halki Palace (Heybeliada).*     *The Shores of Büyükada (above). Orthodox Church in Büyükada (below).*

*The Büyükada Pier.*

Woods and parks cover the hills on the islands where the residences line the northern shores that face the Asian side of Istanbul.

The first island seen from the ferry boat after leaving the pier is the conical shaped, desolate Hayırsız Ada. Next to it is the flat Yassı Ada.

Kınalı Ada is the first inhabited island with a beautiful bay at the back and with beaches opened to the public. An interesting looking modern mosque on the shore attracts the attention. Burgaz, with its rocky beaches, comes after Kınalı. There are watersports clubs on the island. The house of famous Turkish writer Sait Faik Abasıyanık, who used to live on the island, has been turned into a museum. Kalpazankaya, located in the back of the island, is the most popular section of the island.

By the square next to the pier at Heybeli Ada and between the two hills, are the buildings of the Naval School. Beaches occupy its two beautiful coves. The large buildings of the Orthodox Church used to house the school for the monks in the old days. The most popular recreation spot on the island is the Değirmen Park. The Halki Palace hotel, which is one of the two hotels on the island open year round,

was built in the 19th century. In recent years, it was restored and opened for services again. Between Burgaz Ada and Heybeli Ada is a small private island called Kaşık Adası (Spoon Island) due to its shape. Büyükada is the largest, the most popular and the most famous island in the archipelago. It takes two hours to go around the island in a horsedrawn carriage. This island, with high hills, has two public beaches, one of which is in an unusually beautiful cove. The most popular ride on the island follows a course between the mansions in well-kept gardens and through the forests on the hills. In contrast to the heavily populated residential areas near the pier, the back of the island is occupied only by desolate coves and beaches which are ideal harbours for small boats.

Fish restaurants and cafés line the seashore near the pier, and the few hotels and pension houses on the island are found in this area. On weekends and holidays, people crowd the island for picnics and swimming. The small promontory (Dilburnu) on the side of the island facing Heybeli Ada is covered with pine forests and very popular. The Yürükali Beach is on the left side of Dilburnu.

# INFORMATION

**Suggested practical tours outside Istanbul Full Day**

Rented car, private limousine service, or tours organized by travel agencies.

Istanbul-Bursa (One way 220 km.)
Istanbul-Şile (Black Sea coast 66 km.)
Istanbul-Kilyos (Black Sea coast 25 km.)
Istanbul-Princes' Islands
(Büyük Ada 1 hour and half)

**1-night, 2 day tours.**

Istanbul-İznik-Bursa (overnight)
Bursa-Yalova-Princes' Islands-Istanbul
(After Yalova by Ferry)
Istanbul-Tekirdağ-Çanakkale-Troy
(overnight, 330 km.)
Troy-Tekirdağ-Istanbul

**2-day tours by plane/car -outside Istanbul.**

1st day
Istanbul-İzmir-(by plane 50 min.)
İzmir-Bergama 80 km. İzmir (overnight)
2nd day
İzmir-Ephesus etc. (return on late flight)
1st day
Istanbul-Ankara (by plane 45 min.) Trip to Cappadocia by private car (4 hrs) Afternoon orientation tour (overnight)
2nd day
Morning tour-churches-the natural formations-villages
Afternoon-depart for Ankara airport. Return to Istanbul on evening flight
Istanbul-Antalya (the Turkish riviera)
1st day
Istanbul-Antalya (by plane 55 min.).
Then by private car to Perge-Aspendos-Side ruins (overnight)
2nd day
Antalya city tour-museum-return fly to Istanbul

**Classical tours in Turkey.**

(12-14 days, plane/bus/private car)

Leave Istanbul on tours organized by travel agencies, or private groups tours, or by rent-a-car (limousine service).

Istanbul-İznik-Bursa
Bursa-Çanakkale-Troy
İzmir-Ephesus-Kuşadası (2 nights)
Kuşadası-Didim-Priene-Milet-Kuşadası
Kuşadası-Aphrodisias-Pamukkale
Pamukkale-Antalya-Side (2 nights)
Side-Perge-Aspendos-Side
Side-Konya
Konya-Cappadocia (2 nights)
Cappadocia-Ankara (or by plane) Istanbul

**Tour of Eastern Turkey:**

Organized group Tours by bus+plane 11 to 14 days
Istanbul by plane to Trabzon (2 nights)
Trabzon-Sumela Monastery-Trabzon
Trabzon-Erzurum (7 hrs)-Kars.
Border city with Russia. Ruins of old Ani.
Kars-Doğubeyazıt (8 hrs) 5165 mt. Ağrı (Ararat)
Doğubeyazıt-Van (2 nights)
Urartu sites in oasis of East,
Van-tour of Akdamar Island on the Lake-Van.
Van-Diyarbakır (7 hrs) Upper Mesopotamia view. Fantastic walls and mosques.
Diyarbakır-Urfa (4 hrs) visit of Harran, city of prophets.
Urfa-Adıyaman (4 hrs) plain of Fertile Cressent
Adıyaman-Nemrut Dağ-Malatya (13 hours) one of the 8th wonders of the world.
Malatya-Istanbul (by plane 1.30 hrs) or
Malatya-Kayseri-Cappadocia (8 hrs) (2 nights)
Cappadocia sight-seeing
Cappadocia-Ankara (6 hrs)
Ankara-Istanbul (6 hrs)

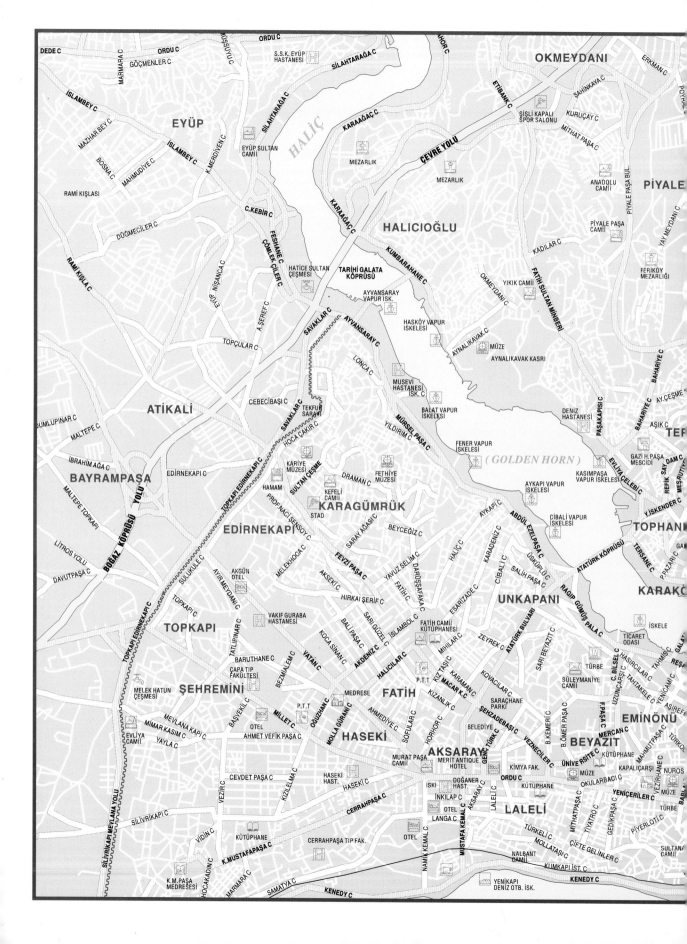

# PUBLICATION LIST

**TURKEY (BN)** *(In English, French, German, Italian, Spanish, Dutch, Japanese, Turkish)*

**ANCIENT CIVILIZATIONS AND RUINS OF TURKEY** *(En Anglais)*

**ISTANBUL (B)** *(In English, French, German, Italian, Spanish)*

**ISTANBUL (ORT)** *(In English, French, German, Italian, Spanish)*

**ISTANBUL (BN)** *(In English, French, German, Italian, Spanish, Japanese)*

**MAJESTIC ISTANBUL** *(En Anglais, German)*

**TURKISH CARPETS** *(In English, French, German, Italian, Spanish, Japanese)*

**TURKISH CARPETS** *(En Anglais, German)*

**THE TOPKAPI PALACE** *(In English, French, German, Italian, Spanish, Japanese, Turkish)*

**HAGIA SOPHIA** *(In English, French, German, Italian, Spanish)*

**THE KARİYE MUSEUM** *(In English, French, German, Italian, Spanish)*

**ANKARA** *(In English, French, German, Italian, Spanish, Turkish)*

**CAPPADOCIA** *(In English, French, German, Italian, Spanish, Japanese, Turkish)*

**CAPPADOCIA (BN)** *(In English, French, German, Italian, Spanish, Dutch)*

**EPHESUS** *(In English, French, German, Italian, Spanish, Japanese, Turkish)*

**EPHESUS (BN)** *(In English, French, German, Italian, Spanish, Dutch)*

**APHRODISIAS** *(In English, French, German, Italian, Spanish, Turkish)*

**THE TURQUOISE COAST OF TURKEY** *(In English)*

**PAMUKKALE** *(In English, French, German, Italian, Spanish, Dutch, Japanese, Turkish)*

**PAMUKKALE (BN)** *(In English, French, German, Italian, Spanish, Turkish)*

**PERGAMON** *(In English, French, German, Italian, Spanish, Japanese)*

**LYCIA (AT)** *(In English, French, German)*

**KARIA (AT)** *(In English, French, German)*

**ANTALYA (BN)** *(In English, French, German, Italian, Dutch, Turkish)*

**PERGE** *(In English, French, German)*

**PHASELİS** *(In English, French, German, Turkish)*

**ASPENDOS** *(In English, French, German)*

**ALANYA** *(In English, French, German, Turkish)*

**The Capital of Urartu: VAN** *(In English, French, German)*

**TRABZON** *(In English, French, German, Turkish)*

**TURKISH COOKERY** *(In English, French, German, Italian, Spanish, Japanese, Turkish)*

**NASREDDİN HODJA** *(In English, French, German, Italian, Spanish, Japanese)*

**ANADOLU UYGARLIKLARI** *(Turkish)*

## MAPS:

**TURKEY (NET), TURKEY (ESR), TURKEY (West)
TURKEY (South West), ISTANBUL, MARMARİS,
ANTALYA-ALANYA, ANKARA, İZMİR, CAPPADOCIA**

## NET® BOOKSTORES

**İSTANBUL GALLERİA BOOKSTORE:**
Galleria Ataköy, Sahil Yolu, 34710 Ataköy Tel: (90-212) 559 09 50
**İSTANBUL MERİT ANTİQUE BOOKSTORE:**
Merit Antique Hotel İçi, Laleli Tel: (90-212) 513 93 00 - 513 64 31
**İZMİR BOOKSTORE:**
Cumhuriyet Bulvarı No: 142/B, 35210 Alsancak Tel: (90-232) 421 26 32